Table of contents

Introduction _____ 9

Changes that college will bring _____ 11

Packing for College _____ 15

    Packing Tips for College _____ 15
        Clothes _____ 16
        Home and Kitchen Gadgets _____ 17
        Home and Laundry Essentials _____ 18

    Making New Friends _____ 21

    Avoiding People _____ 26

    Dealing with Conflict _____ 26

    What to Do When You're Shy _____ 30
        Find Places and People with Similar Interests _____ 30

    What to Do If You're Lonely _____ 32
        Dealing with Homesickness _____ 33
        Dealing with Roommates _____ 34

    Sororities _____ 38

Drink, Drugs, Dating and going out _____ 42

    Drink _____ 42

    Drugs _____ 44

    Dating _____ 45
        Consent matters _____ 46
        Going out _____ 49

    Day-to-Day Survival Tips _____ 52
        Bed _____ 52

    Dealing with Bed bugs _____ 54
        Laundry _____ 56

Food — 66
Food Hacks — 66
Food Delivery Orders — 69
Improve Your Diet — 70
Your Daily Calorie Requirements — 71
How Much of Each Food Group Should You Eat Every Day? — 72

Tips for Busy Students on How to Eat Well — 78
Nutrition Tips — 78
What to Always Have in the Kitchen — 83
Batch Cooking Weekends — 85

Study & exams — 91
Classroom Hacks — 91
Managing Your Schedule — 91
Start the Semester with a Planner — 92
Do not skip class — 94
Where to Sit — 95
Summarize the Lecture — 96
Share Lecture Notes — 99
Choosing a Major — 100
Changing Your College Major — 100
Avoid Cheating and Plagiarism — 101

More Tips — 103
Early to Bed and Early to Rise — 103

Study Hacks and Habits — 107
Where to Start with Studying — 107
Avoid Getting Stressed — 110

Study in Company — 112
Organize a Study Group — 113
Find a Study Buddy — 114

Cost effective on-line materials — 116

Improve Your Memory — 117
Organize Your Notes — 117
Make Associations — 118
Use Visual Cues — 118

College Activities to Try — 121

Health — 122

Sleep _____ 122
Benefits of Sleep _____ 125
Water _____ 131
Eyesight _____ 134
Posture _____ 137
Toothache _____ 138
Skincare _____ 139
Colds, Coughs, and Being Sick _____ 140
   Fresh Fruits _____ 140
   Herbal Teas _____ 140
   Soup _____ 141
First-Aid Tips _____ 142
   Medications _____ 143
Menstruation _____ 144

Exercise _____ *146*
   Higher Levels of Energy _____ 149
   Better Memory _____ 150
   Better Concentration _____ 150
   Improved mood _____ 150
Getting Into Sports _____ 154

Mental Health _____ *155*
   Mindfulness _____ 155
   Meditation _____ 156
   Journaling _____ 156

Technology Hacks _____ *159*
Caring For Your Computer _____ 162
Google Chrome _____ 164
   Ways to Use Google in Searching Information ____ 164
   Creating Folders on the Google Chrome Top Bar __ 170

Money _____ *172*
Managing Your Money _____ 173
   Budgeting and tracking expenses _____ 173
   Savings _____ 176

- How to keep expenses down — 177
- Making Money — 178
- Avoiding Debt — 179
- Student Loans — 180
- Plan Ahead for Debt Pay Off — 181
- Start Investing — 182

Finally — 184

References — 185

Introduction — 190

Part 1: Life skills & living away from home — 192

1. **Renting** — 192
   - Choosing your location — 192
   - Defining your budget — 194
   - Viewing the apartment — 196
   - Signing the contract — 197

2. **Moving in** — 198
   - Buying furniture — 198
   - Cleaning routine — 221

3. **Laundry, house maintenance tips & more** — 227
   - Doing laundry — 227

Part 2: Productivity, health and relationships — 236

1. **Health** — 237
   - The power of self-care — 237

2. **Goal setting** — 248
   - SMART goals — 248
   - Divide and conquer: Goals by areas — 251

3. **Daily routines** — 255
   - Discover your routine — 255

4. **Relationships** — 275
   - Love — 275

5. FAQs and hacks — 284

Part 3: Career & job success — 293

- Finding a job — 293
  - Home office basics — 333

Part 4: Entrepreneurship & money ___ *337*

Money management ___ **337**
The basics of managing money ___ 338
Investing ___ 344
Entrepreneurship ___ 348
USA taxes ___ 357
UK taxes ___ 368
Credit score ___ 370
Debt ___ 372
Savings ___ 378
Buying a house ___ 380
How to choose an insurance plan ___ 384
What's 401k? ___ 386

Part 5: EXTRAS - What you need to know! ___ *387*
What you need to know about your car ___ 387
What you need to know about traveling ___ 394
What you need to know about social media ___ 400

Conclusion ___ *405*

The College Life Survival Guide for Girls

Introduction

Congratulations, you're going to college! The big question is, now what? Maybe you're feeling a bit anxious about how you'll survive on your own, away from your family? Or maybe you're looking for the best advice to be successful and happy in college?

Transitioning to college is a challenge for all students. The transition marks an essential milestone in growing up from teenager to adulthood. This significant step can be both exciting and challenging for you and your family. Moving away to college can be both a scary and amazing experience in a girl's life. The fact is though that your time in college can be one of the best times of your life.

You will be moving away from familiar places and people to a new life filled with new experiences and new people. You will be leaving your childhood behind and taking the first steps in becoming an adult. When you start to think about learning to manage on your own, it can seem like a massive task and like any life change, can cause anxiety as we adapt to our new life.

Some women find the college experience a real struggle, but the good news is that it doesn't have to be! It's no secret that for some students college is a bit of a survival challenge, particularly at first, and this should be recognised. You're in a new city, you don't know many people, your toilet is blocked, your fridge is empty and your exams are looming!

Don't panic! This book is full of advice, hints and tips to help you to prepare and succeed in college. We will share practical tips to help new female college students and soon-to-be female college students to survive and thrive in college. With the proven tips and strategies in this book you'll be able to enjoy the college experience to the full, and come out of college a strong, independent woman, ready for the adult world.

Changes that college will bring

Going away to college is a big change for anyone, but how difficult it is depends on the individual. Moving away from home can be a real challenge for some people because they may not know anyone who is going to the same college. They are leaving school friends behind, and are worried about finding new buddies.

Everyone has a unique experience of leaving home to go to college hours, but college girls often fail to recognize how many of them face the same challenges. Almost everyone is leaving home, everyone is getting used to a new learning environment, everyone is looking to meet new friends.

One of the most challenging aspects of attending college is that so much is unknown. You probably don't know who your roommates will be, what it's like to use a communal bathroom, or what the college workload will be. Most people, even the ones who seem confident, will be feeling unsure about how to live so far away from their home and their friends.

As you stand in line to get your room keys, or wave your parents goodbye after they've dropped off your luggage, the sadness can hit like a brick wall. As you turn your head around to see if you know anyone from the crowd and don't recognize even one, the feeling of anxiety can make you wonder if you made the right decision to make the move.

Maybe you didn't want to leave home because it meant being separated from your family and best friends. You might be leaving activities and clubs behind. You might miss your pets.

On the other hand, you might be eager to get to college, say goodbye to all the rules and regulations you're used to at home and finally enjoy some more freedom.

Whatever your background you may find it difficult to adjust because, at least at first, living outside of your comfort zone can be a challenging experience. The thing to remember in all of this is that college can become your new home, your friends become your new family and you can find new interests.

College can be exciting and challenging at the same time. You can create a ton of memories with new college friends you'll have for life, but on the other hand, professors might swamp you with piles of paperwork – assignments, projects, homework, term papers and case studies that you have to get done on time also.

Whether you intend to live on campus or not, many aspects of your life will change. You will have opportunities to meet new people. You will have more independence and freedom and new responsibilities. College life also brings challenges that can feel overwhelming - but they don't have to be!

Homesickness and loneliness are common experiences, especially for first-year students in college. You may cry over the phone the first time your parents reach out to you, or you may not. None of this is unusual. Don't be embarrassed by whatever emotions you feel and don't feel you should apologize for them. As you become used to college life, you will realize that this was part of the transition to you becoming independent and learning to handle situations on your own.

If you feel lonely, accept that this isn't a failing and understand that you are not alone. Loneliness is something that most new college girls struggle with from time to time. Accept this, accept that you are not alone. This will pass.

The transition to college life is significant, and we don't always anticipate the most challenging aspects. Parents, friends and family frequently sugar-coat the change, claiming that college will be the best time of your life and more. Hopefully it will be, but initially it can feel strange to move to an entirely new environment with completely new people and be expected to become great friends with the people we live with. It is a significant transition, and it's easy to feel that we should hide and bottle up our struggles when we have difficulty adjusting to a new situation. Nobody has to do that.

Awareness of what awaits you can help lessen the impact of stress and anxiety you will be dealing with when separated from your family and familiar things. In this guide will will help you to prepare, covering a lot of topics including:

- Packing preparation
- Making new friends and managing conflicts
- Fighting homesickness
- Day-to-day survival
- Developing healthy eating habits and fitness routines
- Classroom and study difficulties
- Taking care of your mental health

This is your first big step into adult life as a woman. Did you know that 40% of students drop out of college every year in the USA? Well, that's not going to be you, because this book will share with you the proven tips & strategies to make your college days the best days of your life. So let's get started!

Packing for College

When you are going to live away from home for the first time, thinking of what to bring into your new place can be daunting. Don't panic! Put together a list of what you need and use it as a checklist when gathering things together and packing.

Packing Tips for College

If you are staying in the college dorm, expect that you will be sharing your room with someone you haven't met before. You may have a long list of things you want to bring with you, but remember that you won't have a huge space and you can't take the whole house with you!

When thinking of things to include in your list, think of the essentials – only those things you can't live without. Here are some of these:

- Clothes, underwear, shoes, coat
- Sports clothes
- Phone, computer, backup storage, chargers
- Alarm clock, college books,
- Small medical kit
- Bath and toilet essentials

Get a pen and paper, start a list on your phone or open up a blank document on your laptop - whatever works for you get on to that list. Break it down into categories depending on your needs.

Here is an example:

Clothes

When packing clothes, you have to consider the weather conditions depending on the location of the college you are attending. Will you need warm clothes for the winter, or lighter summer clothes? Is your college in a location that gets four seasons in one day?!.

- Shirts – tees, sweatshirts, jackets, cardigans
- Pants – casual, workout, slacks, denim, cozy pants.
- Undergarments – panties, bras

- Nightwear – pajamas or lingerie
- Protective gear – hats, mittens, boots, umbrella
- Shoes – sneakers or running shoes, sandals, and a pair of heels for special occasions
- Belts and bags
- Shorts
- Bathrobes
- House slippers
- Coats - light or heavy

Bedding

- Comforter
- Bed Sheets
- Pillow and Pillow covers
- Duvet

Home and Kitchen Gadgets

- Coffee maker
- Electric kettle
- Mug and cup
- Plates, bowls,
- Rice cooker
- Chopping board
- Condiments organizers

- Drinking glasses
- Plastic food storage
- Eating utensils (2-3 sets)
- Can opener

Home and Laundry Essentials

- Laundry bag
- Laundry detergent
- Stain remover
- Fabric softener
- Disinfectants
- Dishwashing liquid
- Sponges
- Rubber gloves

Toilet, Bath, and Personal Care Essentials

- Soap – facial and body soaps
- Shampoo and conditioner
- Loofah
- Body wash and bath salts
- Body towels
- Shaving cream
- Razors

- Shower shoes
- Moisturizers and facial cleansers
- Toothbrush and toothpaste
- Mouthwash and dental floss
- Sanitary products
- Deodorants
- Nail clippers
- Nail file
- Nail polish
- Nail polish remover
- Hairbrush
- Hairspray
- Curling and straightening iron
- Hair ties, clips, ribbons, etc.
- Cotton pads, cotton swabs, or cotton balls
- Makeup and makeup remover
- Body lotion
- Scissors
- Perfume
- Towels
- Sewing kit

Friends

Making new friends can really help your self-esteem, learning, and academic growth. Having meaningful college friendships during your undergraduate or graduate studies will lead to a better social life and a greater feeling of belonging. It can also be the foundation of a successful and fulfilling education, leading to sought-after employment prospects.

Students who make an effort to build friendships in college are more likely to succeed academically and graduate on time. If you are determined to succeed in your studies you might fall into the trap of spending long hours studying but in the process overlooking the need for social interaction. It is important to put time and effort into your studies but don't let the pressure to succeed overwhelm you to the point that you overlook the need to develop friendships and take time out. Taking a balanced approach to down-time is crucial to success.

Making New Friends

Humans are known to be social animals. We create and foster friendships to have someone to rely on, listen to, or to be there for in times of need— this is how we are.

Friendship allows us to understand, empathize with, and nurture one another. With friends, we bring out the best in one another and can be confident of emotional support during trying times, without the fear of being judged. Good friends will be able to support you when college life feels like hard work, and you will be able to do the same for them.

Studies reveal that college participants who built a close social circle gain social support and academic motivation. These students performed well by studying together, de-stressing regularly, supporting each other in their academic feats, and celebrating their success.

Meanwhile, a lack of friendship and social contact can generate feelings of loneliness, emptiness, and isolation that gradually chip away at emotional well-being.

Of course, building new connections in a melting pot of students from diverse backgrounds and circumstances can be super challenging. While there will be same-age learners like you who start college straight out of high school, there will also be more mature individuals who may be restarting their college life after raising a family or maybe others taking a new career path. These factors, plus the reality that you're still finding your way in a new environment and trying to integrate into new classroom and campus cultures, may at first make it feel hard to make connections.

So, what measures can you use to gain meaningful and powerful connections with good friends during your college years?

In Class

As a rule of the thumb, remember this: You can make more friends by showing interest in other people than by expecting them to be interested in you. If you show that you want to know more about people they will start to open up to you, and then they will want to know more about you.

If building a social network is quite a challenge for you, remember that others at your college or university face the same dilemma as you. They are looking for opportunities to make friends as well.

Whatever new situation you are in, introduce yourself, people will appreciate your effort to reach out to them. A casual conversation with them will help you discover common connections that may start a lifetime of adventure and memorable experiences.

Some classes offer better opportunities to broaden your inner circle. For instance, classes that encourage group activities or projects, no matter how offputting they may feel sometimes, create greater chances for classmates to communicate and build connections. After all, they have more time to talk with each other during these times compared to those classes with straight-up lectures.

On-Campus

Campus events are an incredible way to meet new people. They provide a topic that invites discussion or presents different perspectives (particularly events with guest speakers) and cater to introverts and extroverts alike. Many of these gatherings have a reception before or after. These occasions present attractive opportunities to strike up a conversation.

Thanks to the various social media platforms it's easy to find out what is going on, so engage in social media and on-line notice boards. As you move around campus keep your eyes open for events advertised old-style on posters. You'll probably feel spoiled for choice, as there's probably something going on every night of the week.

Also think about where you might meet new people:

The student center (or the student commons): The building is primarily devoted to student recreation and socialization. Since it often holds student activities, it's a nice place to initiate a casual conversation.

At the gym: If you're working out, you can easily find individuals with a shared interest and start your friendship.

The hall: Waiting in the hall is an open opportunity to meet people who interest you or are interested in you.

Around campus: You might even start up a conversation with someone heading in the same direction as you. If you are shy this might feel like something you'd never do, but you might be surprised at the effect just a smile in someone's direction can have.

In the dormitory: You're likely to spend a lot of time in your dorm, especially during your first year. Dorms are usually packed with students who, like you, are both excited and a little bit scared. They are an excellent venue for spontaneous interaction. Whether you're simply hanging out in the common area doing your assignments, brushing your teeth in the communal bathroom, or doing something fun in the hallway, it doesn't matter, these people are potentially your friends.

If you have roommates, you might want to go together to knock on neighbors' doors to see if they would like to get together. Bringing some snacks or sweets will help you make a good impression. Remember to attend the events hosted by your Resident Assistant. Such informal gatherings are designed to bring your floor's occupants together in a comfortable setting to nurture new relationships.

The above applies to other living conditions (for example, sharing a house or apartment unit with other folks). Even if you live outside the campus, you should always prioritize getting to know your neighbors and room-mates.

Avoiding People

We're not going to dwell on this too much, but it's worth saying that you are perfectly entitled to avoid people who you don't feel comfortable around or who you just don't get on with. It's a fact of life that we won't get on with everyone and that's OK. You can be civil and polite to someone without needing to form a friendship.

Dealing with Conflict

Conflict is unavoidable in life. It can range from simply disagreeing with someone to a full-fledged, long-running feud. As a college student, experiencing conflict is quite normal. After all, a college or a university campus is a common ground for diverse perspectives, values, and beliefs. Sometimes women can lack confidence in standing their ground in these situations. Often men are more vocal and forceful when dealing with conflict.

To handle conflict, here are some valuable suggestions to give you some strategies to consider:

Be accommodating. You might not win an argument, but you can win a friend. This simple (although challenging) decision can protect the peace and be helpful in certain situations. Just be aware that you don't have to be accommodating all the time, your point of view is as important as anyone else's.

Ignore the issue. It might sound counter-intuitive, but it works in some situations, especially ones that aren't worth the effort or critical enough to waste your time and energy on. This approach allows both parties more time to develop a more appropriate solution to address the problem. Sometimes the problem just goes away.

Allow compromises. We have learned this method since we were kids. This approach satisfies both parties as each party must give up something from their side. It reduces tension and stress and serves as an excellent first step for people who aren't yet familiar with each other. Think about what small thing you could compromise on that would satisfy the other party. Consider what they might be able to bend on that would make you feel better as well.

Compete for a resolution. Someone will lose in this zero-sum game, but you must refuse to compromise and insist on resolving the problem. This method is necessary from time to time, mainly when you need to implement a quick solution to an issue. In this situation, you must prioritize what needs to be done over your future relationship with the other party. There is a strategy called The Broken Record Technique that can be very effective in situations where you cannot compromise or change your mind. You can Google for more information on this.

Collaborate to come up with a solution. This approach requires more time, effort, and commitment to resolve an issue. It also necessitates a certain level of trust, allowing both parties to believe that they have a share in the outcome and foster a long-term relationship. Of course, both parties have shared responsibilities for whatever result there might be. In case you need immediate action to resolve a conflict, these suggestions will help you achieve your objective:

- Allow yourself to cool down first to think more carefully about what you need to say and do.
- Discuss it calmly with the other person. They too are presumably looking for a solution.
- Determine the points you can agree on and make this a starting point.

- Rather than focusing on personality, pay attention to behavior and events (for example, "It seems to me that you sometimes leave things disorganized." instead of "You're such a slacker!").
- Always actively listen to the other person's point of view.
- Determine the source of the conflict and ensure that it doesn't get out of hand.
- Create a list of the most critical issues. If you disagree on numerous points, pick one to focus on right now.
- Come up with solutions together. Exert effort to be inventive and experiment with new ideas.
- Always remain respectful and upbeat. Believe in your ability to discover a solution.
- Seek assistance from someone unbiased like your RA, academic advisor or trusted friend.

What to Do When You're Shy

If you're worried about going to college as a shy girl who wants to make more friends, these ideas will help you achieve your goal. It may take some time, but you will eventually find your pals. You could set yourself a goal to do one small thing every day to practise making contact with others.

Find Places and People with Similar Interests

One of the best starting points is to look for opportunities to find people who share your hobbies, interests, and values. Like-minded people attract each other, and because you have a common ground, you will understand each other better and may even create a solid bond to last a lifetime.

Where do you find these potential friends?

Faith-based services and locations: These offer students opportunities for spiritual growth and development through activities, events, and counseling. Many campuses provide multi-faith spaces that cater to students who identify with any religious group. These are also open to those who are spiritual but not religious.

You can also look for opportunities to meet with others of the same faith. By attending church or temple, maybe faith study groups. Since you share the same beliefs and faith, this will increase the likelihood of you finding people you can bond with.

Small sports groups: If you're the type who likes to stay fit, joining a small sports group will help you accomplish two or more of your goals; making friends and keeping your body in shape. A smaller group will feel less daunting because you will only meet a few new people at a time.

Small activity groups: Whether it may be theater and the arts, media and publication, cultural, or the debate club, joining activity groups can introduce you to connections and friendships that go beyond shared interests or passions. As with the small sports groups, you will meet a small number of people at a time.

What to Do If You're Lonely

Finally, dealing with loneliness is a common aspect of college life. If you are lonely, you must take action before you start to feel too bad. As suggested above, you could join a club, a sports team, or a religious organization and participate in their activities. You can attend events hosted by the university. Invite folks to join you for coffee or study sessions. Getting yourself busy will help you avoid feeling lonely.

Sometimes taking active steps can be hard. If that happens be aware that you can reach out to organizations found on the Internet who can offer support. The Verywellfamily website is just one source of advice, the MIND site is also a great resource.

If you have depression or anxiety, don't hesitate to seek help. There's nothing to be ashamed of about what you're going through. With the proper mental health treatment, you'll be able to cope and feel better in no time.

Dealing with Homesickness

Your newfound freedom has a cost, and that's leaving the comforts of your childhood home. The feeling of homesickness happens during transition periods and even after those times. It's akin to the feelings of grief and loss which can occur to anybody, whatever age and in many situations. These feelings don't make you weak, immature, stupid, or abnormal.

It's only natural to miss home, especially during the holidays or winter break. If you're struggling with homesickness, below are some suggestions on how you can generate a sense of home on campus:

- Acknowledge your feeling of homesickness and understand that it is normal and it isn't permanent.
- Set your goals and expectations for your college life.
- Make yourself at home on campus by getting to know your new surroundings.
- Personalize your space with pictures from home.
- Establish daily routines that will help you remove your focus on negative feelings.
- Set new habits that will make your new environment feel like home.

- Seek opportunities to build your social network on campus.
- Participate in community service programs as a volunteer.
- Look for a spiritual or religious group.
- Maintain communication with family and friends. Reach out to them for support and let them know how you feel.

Finding people with whom you can connect and develop a sense of belonging is crucial in college. One of the most incredible things about experiencing college life is the opportunity to be a part of something bigger than yourself.

Dealing with Roommates

Living with a new person can be an excellent way to branch out of your comfort zone and meet new people. It could also be a massive challenge for you because adjusting to something new requires spending energy. Sharing space can be interesting to say the least. You might find your roommate getting on your nerves from time to time. On the flip side, your newfound relationship may lead to a beautiful friendship that lasts a very long time.

When you feel uncertain about how to handle this new shared setup, below are some suggestions for sharing a room:

Get acquainted with your roomie. It is the first and most important rule in living with someone. Find out the basics, such as what interests and irks them, as well as what their boundaries are. Naturally, you won't be "besties" in an instant, but remember that this person will spend a lot of time with you, so it's only wise and fair to get to know them.

Communicate. Communication is vital in any relationship. Tell your roommate everything they should know about you and your suggestions about your setup. Take this opportunity to set your boundaries and talk about your shared responsibilities. It is also preferable to tell them if anything is bothering you before it transforms into a full-blown argument. Bear in mind that things might not all go according to your plans, when you're sharing a room compromise is usually necessary.

Familiarize yourself with each other's schedules. Their timetable determines many things that may affect both of your performances. Let's say you are a night owl and the other person is an early bird. Your nightly activities might disturb them, just as their morning movement sounds could interrupt your sleep. Sit down and talk about this and work out how you can both make things easier for each other. Bear in mind that if you know your roomie's routine you will quickly notice if something seems wrong, for example if they don't come home one night when they planned to. They will be able to do the same for you.

Be respectful. Part of being respectful is being considerate and open-minded. Your roommate may come from a different background or culture, which may mean that they have different values. Your habits and personalities might well be different, but try to meet in the middle to avoid conflict. For instance, always check with your roommate when you want to invite friends over or when you need to do something that might disturb them. Always ask their permission when you want to borrow something.

Invest in headphones. Your headphones don't merely deter unwanted interruptions but they can also help maintain silence and peace in your room. While you and your roomie may share the same taste in music, movies, or TV series, that doesn't permit you to blast the volume of whatever you're watching or listening to for them to hear. Wear your headphones whenever you go sound-tripping or binge-watching.

Be nice. Even if your new roommate isn't the most amiable person you've ever met or you have contrasting personalities, play it nice. The mood in the room and your interaction with them can significantly impact your new lifestyle and academic performance.

Give them some breathing space. Personal space can become a significant concern with roommates. Transitioning into a smaller living area can be inconvenient, and sharing your place with another person can make it even more challenging. Leave your roommate a few hours in the room to themselves each week, and they will hopefully reciprocate.

Sororities

A sorority is a college campus organization whose goal is to build a sense of camaraderie and community, among other things. Women join a sorority, whereas men join a fraternity.

Each sorority group has its own goals, rules, and expectations. You can join a sorority if you demonstrate that you possess the qualities that meet their specific requirements. The attributes they are looking for are usually based on your personality, academic achievements, community involvement, and campus engagement. The process of recruiting sorority members is called a rush. During the process of getting to know sorority members the potential recruits are called rushees. Bear in mind that sorority sisters will vote at the end of the process to decide which rushees can join them, so nothing is a done deal. Don't on any account be demoralized if you don't end up in your first choice sorority, it doesn't change who you are.

Many first-year college students want to join a sorority or fraternity because it creates a sense of social integration and enables them to build relationships and friendships, however it's not an essential part of college life.

What are the benefits of joining a sorority?

Academics

Most sororities set a minimum GPA requirement, encouraging you to focus on your studies and perform well in your coursework. If your GPA goes too low after you've been initiated, the sorority will place you under probation.

But it isn't all doom and gloom. Sororities encourage sisters to learn together. Hence, study groups and rooms are frequently rented exclusively for sorority sisters.

Campus Involvement and Influence

You'll learn to be a leader on campus, a skill that will also come in handy in your future profession.

Sorority and fraternity members actively participate in many organizations, such as the student government, student affairs, and other student-led societies. Participating in extracurricular activities can help you improve your curriculum vitae for job applications, summer employment, and internships after graduation.

Charitable Endeavors

Many sororities are involved in philanthropy and charity works. As a result, you'll be expected to participate in these events and get more interested in charity.

You may be required to not only participate in these activities as a member of a sorority but also to organize them. Members frequently assist in registering people for various charitable organizations, planning fundraising events, and managing the "Philanthropy Day" for the sorority.

Social and Professional Connections

Joining a sorority is also one of the most effective methods to broaden your career options. Active alumni of your sorority who are frequently recruiting prefer sisters from their sorority group, so staying active in your sorority after college is a good option.

You'll have a lifelong social network, friends with whom you share deep personal connections, and professional benefits. These are vital relationships since your sorority sisters will always be there to support, encourage, and celebrate with you.

Hazing and initiation

You will be aware that in the past, particularly in fraternities, there have been some pretty awful hazing and initiation rituals. To a certain extent this happened in some sororities as well. These rituals were humiliating and sometimes dangerous and colleges have taken action to stop them now. This means that you are very unlikely to be subjected to anything similar if you pledge to join a sorority. However, in the event that you find yourself in any situation where you do not feel comfortable - be strong and walk away. In all of your time in college only take part in things that you want to, and that you feel comfortable with.

Drink, Drugs, Dating and going out

You should be able to look back on college as a time when you were able to enjoy a new-found freedom, build friendships and maybe a special relationship. It's a fantastic time to be young and filled with energy and ideas. However it would be wrong to avoid mentioning some of the pitfalls that you may encounter.

Drink

We tend not to think of alcohol as a drug but of course it can be just as much of a problem as anything else. It can be addictive, it can make us lose control of our actions and can compromise our health.

Firstly, the legal age to drink will depend on what country you live in. For some it's 18 years of age. For others, it's 21 years of age. Being realistic, there aren't many college students who don't get carried away a little in the excitement of a good party. It would be great if the following massive hangovers would put them off repeating the performance, but that is generally not the case. Take responsibility for yourself, and stay strong. If you decide to drink alcohol, be moderate and stop as soon as you start to feel the effects. You went to college for a reason, which is to study and get the qualifications you need to set you up for the rest of your life. Don't compromise that for the sake of getting drunk. You need to be bright and ready to work in the mornings, not fighting a hangover and feeling queasy (or worse!). Remember that regular misuse of alcohol can lead to alcoholism, a terrible addiction, and can damage your body.

Whatever you drink when you are out there is a safety issue that all girls need to be aware of. That is that sometimes drinks get spiked. Rohypnol and GHB are two of the most common "date rape" drugs. If you are unfortunate enough to drink these down you will quickly start to lose control of your body and become disorientated. So keep your drink with you. If you need to go to the lavatory, have a friend keep your drink with them. If you realize that you have left your drink for a while maybe it's safer to just abandon it and go get another. It's sad that we have to think this way, but we do.

Drugs

We could write pages on the dangers of drugs to try to persuade new college students to avoid drugs, but the message is simple - just don't. Don't risk your health, your studies and your personal safety for any sort of high.

Drugs can be dangerous in their own right, and they are sometimes contaminated. Drugs can and do kill students every year. It's just not worth it.

It's almost certain that at some time in your college career you will be offered drugs. Be aware that this doesn't always happen in a social setting, students use drugs to help themselves to stay awake for studying, and to help them to sleep. If you do your best to have a healthy lifestyle, if you plan your timetable to study sensibly, you don't need drugs to get through college. When you're out socializing you can have a great time without taking anything to try to enhance your mood.

Be the strong one who stays in control of life without relying on mind-altering plants or chemicals.

Dating

Most students will date while they are in college and go through all the emotional highs and lows that come with that. It can be a great distraction from studies but we're only human and just have to work our way through it! Here are some things you might want to bear in mind:

Most guys are good guys and just as nervous and uncertain about dating someone new as we are. There are some bad apples out there though, so be ready for that. This advice applies if your date is female as well of course.

Until you get to know your date a bit better, tell a friend where you are going and who you are going with. Have an arrangement to ring them at a certain time to confirm you are back in your room and a plan to contact them if you aren't. Be reliable about this, if you're running late make sure your friend knows. If you don't follow the arrangements they will stop bothering to check.

For first dates, meet in a public place. If you feel that you don't want to take things any further, be polite and don't be afraid to leave.

On the other hand, if you think things are going great you might want to still avoid going off to a more private place, decline any invitations to go back to the guy's room. Expect to be respected. There's no need to rush anything.

If you get to a more intimate stage in your relationship this might sound obvious - but when the time comes use a barrier form of protection and consider using secondary birth control such as the pill as well. Getting pregnant isn't the only thing that can go wrong. There are a variety of sexually transmitted infections and diseases that can be caught. Heterosexual people can and still do catch HIV.

Depending on your chosen method, you might need consent from a guardian if you are still a minor. It's essential to be aware of the laws where you live.

Consent matters

Never, ever feel that you have to do anything that you are not comfortable with in a relationship. You do not have to try something new to "see if you like it" when you are pretty sure that you won't. Sex should never feel demeaning, it should never make you feel unhappy, it should never leave you in pain. It should be an intimate and joyful sharing between two people.

However much you feel you love someone, if they are trying to persuade you to do something that you don't want to - walk away. If they are trying to force you to do anything - leave immediately.

If someone does something to you against your will, without your consent, it is rape. It doesn't have to be full sex, it can be a sexual act caried out against your will. It is rape even if it happens in what appears to be a loving relationship.

If someone forces themselves on you in any situation, whether it be at a party or in your own room, it is rape. If you were unable to consent because you were under the influence of drink or drugs that doesn't change anything. Whatever the situation you are not to blame, the person who committed the act is.

If you are ever in a situation where you are unfortunate to have suffered a physical or sexual assault please do not keep it to yourself. Seek support from a trusted friend, go straight to an adult in authority and get help.

Pregnancy

Sometimes life takes a turn that you never wanted or expected. If you think that you might be pregnant don't put off taking action, or lay awake at nights wondering if you are - take a test and find out.

If you are pregnant it is very important that you act quickly to get advice and consider your options. There will be challenging times ahead and difficult decisions to be made. Talk to someone you trust, or if you feel more comfortable with someone who doesn't know you at first, speak to your doctor or contact a local, independent pregnancy advice service. If you do not want to continue with a pregnancy then unfortunately you will need to be advised on the legal implications in the state where you live.

Going out

Following on from all of this advice, don't let it worry you too much, just bear it all in mind to make sure that you stay safe and enjoy college life.

Don't go out alone at night on campus or elsewhere. Buddy up with someone for company and safety. Women should feel safe to walk anywhere at any time but we know that sadly there are low-lifes out there who will prey on lone women, so we say take a pragmatic approach.

If you are on a night out on the town, or at a party with friends you need to look out for each other. There needs to be a rule that no girl is ever left behind. Talk about this with your friends so that everyone is on the same page. Bear in mind that if your friend is behaving strangely they could be under the influence of drugs or alcohol and need you to intervene and take them home. If you and your group all do this you will stay safe on your nights out.

Any time you are out and you feel uncomfortable don't be embarrassed to act. If a guy is harassing you ask for help from bar staff or your friends. If you start to feel dizzy and disorientated again, tell someone, let them know that you need help. Don't be led away from your friends and the crowd, speak up if you ever feel you are losing control.

When you're taking a cab just take a moment to look at the car and make sure it's not a private vehicle. It's a good idea to travel with company, but if you are alone there is nothing to stop you taking a photo of the car on your phone and sending it to a friend. A genuine cab driver won't mind and will understand why you feel the need to do that.

Following these tips will help you to enjoy the varied and exciting college social life with your new found friends.

College Life

Maybe you have longed for this for the longest time: **Independence**. However, it is easy to underestimate the responsibilities of living alone. Though it may seem trivial, on top of studying, on and off-campus activities, and other social activities you are going to have to deal with daily chores.

It's likely that at home you did some of the chores and housework but not all of them. It's entirely different when you are living independently since you must do every chore yourself, or with help from a roommate.

You will be responsible for everything - including making your bed, laundry, cooking, organizing, and budgeting, among many other things. Now is when you realize that freedom always comes at a price. So don't wait until it's all too much and you don't know what to tackle first, have plans in place from the start.

Day-to-Day Survival Tips

Consider the following pointers to establish a system that will help you manage your daily routine effortlessly. Set up a timetable of chores to be done and try to stick to it. Include your roommate in your plans if you share.

Bed

In the past, you might have tried every excuse not to make your bed every morning. No matter how trivial it may seem, this task signifies consideration and respect for yourself and your roommate if you have one.

No, you don't have to expend much energy to make your bed Pinterest or Instagram-worthy. Fluffing your pillows and flattening your comforter and bed sheet should be enough.

We spend an average of eight hours every day in bed. During that time we sweat and dead skin cells, dirt, body oils, and other grime accumulate on our sheets and bedding. This can cause allergies, acne, and other skin problems and on top of that, it can't contribute to a restful night's sleep.

Make sure that your bed linens are washed once a week and incorporate this into your plan for chores.

The benefits of making our beds every morning are as simple as having a nice comfortable bed to fall into at night. But a tidy bed is the start of a tidy room. A tidy room gives you an organized and comfortable space to study in without distractions.

If washing your linens once a week or more regularly isn't an option, there are a few things you have to do to extend the duration between washes. For one, take a shower before bedtime to limit the amount of sweat, oil, and grime you bring into bed with you. Remove your makeup (which will also avoid some eye problems). Don't eat anything in bed, and never wear your shoes in bed.

Make sure that your pillows are washable and to keep them soft and fluffy wash them every three to five months.

Comforters and Blankets

Comforters and throw blankets don't need to be frequently washed since they have less contact with your skin. Be extra careful when washing your quilt or blanket. Your method should depend on what material they are made from. Check the wash label and follow the instructions.

Heavier blankets and quilts are best left in the care of Laundromats since commercial-sized machines are specially designed to handle them better.

Electric blankets: Heated blankets are designed to be machine washable but follow the manufacturer's instructions to the letter. Failure to do that can make your electric blanket unsafe.

Dealing with Bed bugs

Unfortunately, bed bugs hitch rides in clothing and suitcases in all parts of the world. This means that, with so many people coming together from all parts of the world, colleges are one of the most common places where bed bug infestations are found. So it's worth us spending some time advising on how to deal with them. The first thing to know about bed bugs is that they don't mean that a place is dirty. Bedbugs travel about on luggage and clothing and are happy to set up home in the best four star hotel or the smallest apartment.

Usually the first sign of bedbugs is that someone will get bitten and blood can be seen on bedding. If in doubt you can Google for pictures of typical bedbug bites. They spread quickly, so you have to deal with them immediately. However, eliminating is no easy feat and you should not attempt it yourself. If you believe your room has bed bugs, it's critical to inform your RA immediately. Do not, by any means, douse your room with toxic sprays or "bombs". Doing this is far more dangerous than bed bug infestation. Your RA will make sure the situation is dealt with properly.

To avoid getting bedbugs in the first place, here are some strategies to follow:

- After you have been on vacation, and before packing for college, vacuum your suitcases and bags.
- Take a large trashbag on holidays and keep your suitcase in it during hotel stays.

- Familiarize yourself with how the signs of bed bugs look and check your furniture and bags regularly, using a flashlight.
- If you see any signs of blood on your sheets immediately check for bedbugs.
- Thoroughly check any second hand furniture, baggage or soft furnishings before bringing them into your accommodation.

As always, you can find more detailed information on the Internet.

Laundry

A lot of students have never done any laundry before going to college. Even if you're used to doing laundry at home, you will find that using a college laundry room is an entirely different experience.

Check out the cost of using the campus washers and dryers. Some are free, some accept quarterly installations, and others accept electronic payment via your campus debit card or a prepaid laundry card. Whatever it is, just make sure you have the correct payment method before you run out of clean clothes. Then plan out your laundry schedule and add it to your chores plan.

Carefully Plan Your Laundry Routine

The worst possible time to do your laundry is when you're in a rush, you don't have anything clean to wear, and there's a long waiting line to use the machines. Although each campus is unique, the best possible times to do your laundry are the weekday afternoons and during major events. Expect laundry rooms to be super busy during the evenings and weekends. Also, take advantage of the college or university app that notifies you when washers are available.

Always Sort Your Laundry

It's easier to sort your laundry before you go to the laundry room than try to do it when you get there and may be limited for space.

Group the items by colors and fibers since you don't want your whites smudged with black and your fabrics to shrink or wrinkle. Sort them into groups of white, light, and dark colors or based on how delicate their fabric is. Having a look at the garment care labels, this will help a lot. Generally your laundry will either be delicate or more robust, dark items and whites.

If you only have a few items for a wash load either save them until you have a full load or hand-wash them.

Remember - if you wash coloured items with light items you might find that the colours have run and ruined your best white shirt! If you wash a lovely woolen jumper on a hot setting it might come out just the right size for a five year old child!

We don't want to be boring about laundry so in brief our advice is - Don't forget to read the laundry labels and do what they say.

Determine the Load

Figuring out how much one laundry load is in a new machine can be tricky, especially if it's your first time doing the laundry in your campus laundry room. To determine the load, fill the washer halfway with soiled clothes without stuffing it. This will serve as a guideline. Then, put the load back to your hamper or laundry basket. The amount of clothes inside the basket is the amount you need to put inside the washer for every load. To avoid forgetting this, you could take a photo of the hamper or basket with the measured load.

Check out your surroundings

People aren't great at keeping laundry rooms clean and tidy. Before you spread out your laundry check the surfaces to make sure there isn't detergent or bleach that may permanently damage your clothes.

Inspect inside the machines as well. Look out for items left inside. If you see that the machine is dirty, the easiest thing is probably to clean it. If you're not sure, notify the laundry room manager about the issue.

Don't Forget to Place Labels

Sometimes things get muddled up in the campus laundry room. Labeling your laundry items, such as your detergent, fabric softener and laundry bags, is a good way to avoid disputes about ownership.

Be Mindful When Using a Dryer

First, never use a dryer without a lint trap or filter. Before starting the dryer, you must also ascertain that the lint trap is clean. In doing so, you'll avoid fires, and your garments will dry more quickly. Many commercial dryers default to run on hot cycles, so make it a point to check out the temperature setting before drying your clothes.

Commercial dryers tend to be larger than household ones. You may be able to fit two loads into one machine. As you load your wet laundry into the machine, give each item a brisk shake to fluff it up. This way, the garment will dry faster and have a lesser possibility of having wrinkles. Double-check everything before starting the machine. Keep in mind that opening and closing the door means losing heat and time.

Tips on Getting Rid of Stains

If you happen to experience a mishap, the following will save you from frustration and losing your favorite clothes:

Sweat, Vomit, and Other Bodily Fluids

You need enzyme laundry detergent and oxygenated non-chlorine bleach. The former breaks down the proteins, making it easier to remove the stain. Wash the garment using the hottest setting recommended for the fabric. If an undesirable odor remains even after washing, rewash the garment with a laundry detergent designed to fight odors.

Blood Stains

Firstly, soak the stained garment in cold water, gently rubbing the part with the stain to remove as much blood as possible. If the water turns reddish, replace it continually until it turns clear. Rinse the garment and apply an enzyme laundry detergent (a stronger one if possible). Let it soak for a while to let the stain remover do its work. If the detergent isn't enough, apply a small amount of oxygenated non-chlorine bleach directly to the spot, but be careful as it may be corrosive to some fabrics (i.e., delicate fabrics such as silk and wool).

Red Wine

Cover the stain with salt since it will absorb the wine's color (you will see that the salt will turn pink). Immerse the garment in cold water with enzyme laundry detergent overnight. If needed, repeat the process until the stain is removed and wash the garment as usual.

Fruit and Fruit Juice

Run cold water over the stained spot to dilute the stain. Directly apply an enzyme laundry detergent to the stain, ensuring it is covered completely. Allow it to soak for around 20 minutes. Do not rinse the detergent; wash the garment at the hottest temperature applicable to its fabric.

Coffee

Put the stained spot under cold running water to dilute the stain, and cover it with enzyme laundry detergent. Brush the area with a soft-bristled brush (an old toothbrush, if you may) to ensure that the detergent works on the stain. Set it aside for about five to eight minutes before washing it as usual.

Ink

Put a scrap fabric or paper town underneath the stained spot. Spritz some hairspray on the stain and let it sit for a few seconds. Use a clean paper towel or cloth to blot away the excess ink. Redo the process until the ink stain is entirely gone, then wash the garment as usual.

Grease

Grease-fighting dishwashing liquid does wonders to any grease stain. First, rinse the stain by running cold water over the stain. Apply the dishwashing liquid and rub the spot to loosen the stain. Rinse and repeat the process if necessary.

Gently rub a laundry detergent (use a more powerful stain-fighting type if the grease is from motor oil) into a stain. Saturate the greased area with the soap, and let it sit for about ten minutes or longer. Without rinsing, run the garment in the washer with the hottest possible setting applicable for the garment.

Tomato

Put liquid detergent directly into the stain and rub it with your fingers. Rinse and repeat the process as many times as needed. If the stain lingers, apply an enzyme laundry detergent to the tomato stain and let it stand for about 20 minutes or more. Without rinsing the detergent, run the garment in the washer with the hottest possible setting the fabric can handle.

Mud

Allow the mud to dry and carefully scrape the excess off. Cover the stain with laundry detergent and add a little water. Rub the fabric until the soil is reduced. Rinse and redo the process until the stain is completely gone.

For colorfast fabrics, use a mixture of equal parts water and vinegar if the stain is not removed during the first attempt. Let it stand for a while and wash the garment with enzyme laundry detergent.

Tips in Ironing Clothes

The following recommendations will help you accomplish your ironing task without any hassle:

- Always follow label instructions (see ironing symbols and meanings above).
- Make sure that your ironing board is a well-padded one. If it doesn't have adequate padding, buy a board cover with padding. You can also add extra padding by placing an old but clean blanket.
- Use distilled water when steaming because it prolongs the life of your iron.
- When ironing in bulk, start with items that require lower temperature, then work your way to items that require a higher setting.
- You can eliminate stubborn wrinkles by misting the wrinkled part with water before ironing. A spray bottle works well to accomplish this.
- When hanging clothes, button up to the second button from the top to hold the dress, blouse, or shirt in place.
- Iron fragile, synthetic, and thick fabrics on the wrong side. Apply this method to your outfits with graphics to avoid melting the designs.
- Let the iron cool down for at least 30 minutes before storing it.

Folding Clothes

You will probably have a lot less space for your clothes than you had at home. Folding your clothes tidily will mean that they fit into less space than if they were just thrown in. You can get some handy gadgets to organize your clothing and save space, like shoe racks for the bottom of the closet, and clothes hangers that take more than one shirt.

There are many videos on social media showing great hacks for folding and rolling clothes to store them when space is limited. Maybe have a look.

Food

When you are living independently you have complete freedom in what you will eat. However, keep in mind that in every kind of freedom, there also comes responsibility. It's your responsibility to ensure that you stay healthy. It might be fun to eat pizza and donuts for the whole week, but it's not healthy.

College students have a limited budget, shared kitchen and busy schedules, making most meal plans look impractical and expensive. Ideally you would cook nutritious meals all of the time, but in practice that won't happen.

Food Hacks

Listed below are some healthy tips that will help you in your college life.

Choose Your Food Wisely

Eating healthy will look different for every college student, so it's necessary to find options that will work for you. As you make friends you'll also want to consider their food preferences, intolerances and maybe even allergies. You might need to consider the difference between vegetarians and vegans. Gluten and dairy intolerance - it's a long list. The most important thing to start with is to make a healthy meal plan that suits you.

You can still have tasty treats and the occasional junk food meal of course. But limit the chips and eat carrot batons instead. Have fruit to hand to eat when you crave something sweet, don't always turn to Oreos and cakes from the deli. Remember if you don't buy the sweet things you can't eat them, so avoid stocking up on them.

Keep a Three-Day Food Journal and Analyze It

Planning your meal is an excellent way to eat a healthy diet, even on a budget. For every meal, add two fruits or vegetables. For example, you might include banana, orange, or avocado in your breakfast.

You can use your food journal to create meal plans. Meal plans will not only help you to eat healthily, they will help you to save money. Instead of drifting around the food hall picking up items at random you will take what you know you need for the next few days.

For most college students it works to plan at least three days of healthy eating, followed by one 'free day,' when they can eat whatever they like. Then they follow another three day meal plan and so on.

Filling In Your Journal

Write down the list of foods you might want to eat or drink for three days. Once done, note how many portions you can eat from those. For example, if your appetite allows you to eat three ham sandwiches during breakfast, write three servings.

You can also write the list of condiments that you usually consume with your food, e.g., ketchup, mayonnaise, soy sauce, etc. Include notable condiments in your meal plans since you still need to buy them.

If you also eat fast food, kindly indicate how much you will eat their meals or how frequently you go to their chains to eat.

Write your daily activities, including workouts, travels, and mood. After all, our mood affects our eating habits since food is well-known to improve one's mood whenever we get stressed. Make sure to keep track of your activities as much as possible.

Food Delivery Orders

With the advent of technology, life is getting more convenient for everyone, including college girls, because of the growing trend in food delivery. It's easier now to order food online and have them delivered instead of dining out for a traditional meal.

USA Today recently revealed that 77% of millennials use a food delivery service. It is 26% more than all the diners in the United States (Sun, 2018). Because of the growing trend, apps like *Menufy* are now taking care of your food needs via online ordering. Here are some tips to consider for making your online food-ordering service a better experience.

Order Food Early

Plan when you don't intend to cook because of your hectic schedule. When you opt for online food delivery, make sure you order early, so it's ready when you're home. You might leave instructions to the driver to leave your delivery in a designated place.

Food ordered online can be unhealthy, but it doesn't have to be, there are plenty of healthy options available too.

Improve Your Diet

With free access to late-night food delivery and dining halls with buffets, it's no wonder that so many college students gain weight.

In their first year on campus, one in every four freshmen gained ten pounds or more, according to a study of their diets. Those who gained weight ate fewer fruits and vegetables and more fatty foods and slept less than those who didn't gain weight (Sun, 2018).

Poor eating is also linked to getting lower grades, getting sick more often, and feeling more tired. There is also a higher chance of depression, anxiety, irritability, trouble focusing, and trouble sleeping.

Fast food and unhealthy snacks don't give you the nutrition you need to do well in school. Having a healthy, balanced diet from a young age can help you do better in school and get you into a habit of healthy eating.

You probably learned about the primary food groups and the food pyramid when you were still a child. The iconic pyramid created in 1992 became a symbol of healthy eating. It was integrated into the school curriculum and widely used in elementary school cafeterias for more than 20 years.

But in 2014, the U.S. Department of Health got rid of the food pyramid and replaced it with a new picture called *MyPlate*. *MyPlate* shows how much of each of the five primary food groups you should eat instead of how many servings you should eat.

MyPlate says that fruits and vegetables should make up about half of your diet. It likewise tells people to eat less dairy and grains than the original food pyramid said they should.

Your Daily Calorie Requirements

In 1992, the USDA said that most adults should eat about 2,000 calories per day. But because of new research, the

USDA now says that most of us don't need 2,000 calories every day. Also, the department says we should eat more vegetables and fewer grains. People of different ages, sizes, and physical activity levels can have very different calorie and portion size needs. An NFL linebacker should eat about 3,500 calories on game day, but a college sophomore working on a term paper might only need half of that.

Even between the ages of 19 and 30, the recommended daily intake for men and women is nearly 20% different.

How Much of Each Food Group Should You Eat Every Day?

Knowing how each food group affects your body can determine what you should eat and how much. Let's go back to review what we had learned about nutrition and healthy eating.

Grains

Women should eat between 6 and 8 ounces of grains every day, while men should eat 8 to 10 ounces.

Whole grains and refined grains are the two types of grains that people can buy. Adding whole grains to our diets makes us less likely to have heart problems, and we need fibers to aid us in our digestion.

Whole grains make you feel fuller. You'll feel full faster and eat healthier than if you eat refined or enriched grains.

Protein

Women should eat 5–6.5 ounces of protein every day, while men should get between 6.5-7 ounces of protein daily.

Protein is an integral part of what makes up the human body. We need it to keep our muscles, bones, blood, skin, and joints healthy. Protein turns calories into energy in its most basic form.

It's essential to get protein from healthy sources. Unfortunately, many high-protein foods are also high in cholesterol and saturated fats or made from trans fats and other harmful ingredients. Choose lean or plant-based proteins whenever you can to protect your heart health.

You should eat between 45 and 55 grams, or about six ounces, of protein every day, depending on your body type. Since most Americans eat a lot more protein than they need, this amount may seem low at first.

Dairy

Women should drink three cups of milk every day, while men should drink three cups of milk every day.

Dairy's main benefit is calcium, which helps our bones and teeth stay healthy. Dairy products include anything with milk, but it's essential only to count dairy that keeps its calcium content. Even though cream cheese and butter are made from milk, they are not in this group. Dairy products are things like natural cheeses, yogurt, and milk in any form.

You should include low-fat or fat-free dairy in your daily diet. College students should eat about 3 cups of dairy every day. It might be as easy as drinking a couple of glasses of milk.

Fruits and Veggies

Fruits and veggies are women's best friends. Consume at least four to five cups of fruits and vegetables daily, while men should eat five to five and a half cups of fruit and vegetables every day.

Fruits and vegetables are full of good things for your body, such as potassium, fiber, vitamin C, and folate. They are also low caloric content and have no cholesterol, which is good for you if you wish to maintain a healthy weight.

You need fiber to help lower blood pressure and cholesterol, keep your bowels working well, and improve your heart health. Fiber-rich foods make us feel full. College students should try to eat about two and a half to three cups of vegetables and two cups of fruit every day. This is the same as 12 baby carrot sticks, a good-sized salad, and two small pieces of fruit.

Fruit and Veggie Subgroups

Some nutritionists divide this food group further into subgroups based on the color of the fruit or vegetable: red, orange, green, blue, or white. To improve your diet, try to eat something from each of these groups every day as plants with bright colors also contain a lot of vitamins. It's also beneficial to remember that raw fruits and vegetables have more bulk and fiber. Cooked vegetables can be just as healthy, but you'll need to eat more to reach your daily goal.

Reconsider Your Appliances

Because you don't have a full kitchen during your stay in college, you will need to consider what appliances are practical in your room. Examine your kitchen appliances and reconsider them. Morning smoothies can be made with a single-serving blender. A juicing sieve can be used to make cold-pressed juice. You can make fresh almond butter for breakfast using raw almonds and coconut oil.

You can make delicious hummus with garbanzo beans to serve with pita bread or fresh vegetables. Cauliflower mash also works well. Cook your cauliflower in the microwave using a microwave-friendly package. Blend in the cheese, seasonings, and a splash of milk. It's tasty and a great way to get some extra vegetables.

Most dorm rooms have a toaster, at least. It would make delicious toast, but it would also be ideal for warming *naan* for open-faced pizzas or filling pitas with hummus, veggies, and feta cheese. A plate of bruschetta is a tasty go-to quick dinner. Just make some topping using a few ingredients and serve it on whole-wheat toast.

Prepare Your Snacks

When studying late at night and getting hungry, try to avoid getting tempted to eat candy, chips, or treats from a vending machine. Unbuttered popcorn, fresh or dried fruit, pretzels, rice cakes, or whole wheat crackers are excellent options. Try raw vegetables with low-fat yogurt or cottage cheese dip if you have a fridge.

Limit Your Daily Caffeine Consumption

Can you limit your coffee time to just one cup per day? A glass of tea will suffice if you have a late-night studying ahead of you.

Caffeine is hard on your skin and can make you irritable if you sit for long periods. It can become addictive and cause cravings. Carry a more healthy alternative with you, such as a bottle of flavored water. Drink whenever you feel tired of your body to feel revitalized and alert.

Tips for Busy Students on How to Eat Well

The average college student is often short on time, under a lot of stress, and eating on the go. You might find it hard to break bad habits like skipping meals or going to fast food places. But eating well can make you feel better, help you deal with stress, and help you do better in school and sports. After all, it's easy to get started.

Nutrition Tips

Eat breakfast well. Studies prove that skipping breakfast makes it harder to do well in school. Suppose you don't have time to sit down and eat breakfast, grab a bagel, a piece of fruit, and a glass of juice. Most of these things are easy to store in your room in the dorm.

Eat lots of calcium-rich foods. Those in their early 20s need to build up their calcium stores to avoid osteoporosis later. If you don't like milk, try to eat a lot of low-fat yogurts, low-fat cheese, and green leafy vegetables.

Limit how much sugar you eat. Sugar gives you calories but not many other nutrients and it causes tooth decay. Use it in small amounts and think about using sweeteners instead.

Eat healthy rather than diet. Starvation and quick-fix diets don't work long term and can be harmful. If you feel that you need to lose weight start by cutting out the sweets, treats and alcohol and eating healthily. You might be surprised by the results. Add in some regular exercise and see how you feel in six months time, we're sure you'll feel better!

Go to the salad bar in the dining hall. Depending on your choice, the salad bar in the dining hall can help or hurt your diet. Raw and green leafy veggies plus fresh fruits are all good for you. But if you love to have a lot of creamy dressings, bacon bits, and mayonnaise with your salads, bear in mind that calorie and fat content may be the same or even higher than what you would eat in burgers and fries, so choose wisely.

Drink plenty of water. Human beings need at least eight glasses of water a day; if you work out hard, you may need even more. Keep a water bottle anywhere you go and keep it nearby when studying late at night.

Limit how much alcohol you drink. If you drink alcohol, remember it gives you calories but nothing else. About 100 calories are in a light beer, wine, or an ounce of liquor. There are also health risks associated with alcohol.

Have fun eating. Food is more than just fuel for our bodies, so take the time to enjoy and savor it.

Visit Your Doctor

To know if you have any nutritional deficiencies, get a check up with your healthcare provider. You may have your blood checked to determine your state of health. If you have any deficiencies in iron, B12, Vitamin C, etc., you may augment your nutrition through meal preparation or take food supplements to meet your nutritional requirements.

Shopping Tips

Staying healthy and being on track with their budget can be challenging for college students. However, there are tips to follow to make your college life more convenient, beneficial, and right on the budget.

Have a Plan

You can't go beyond your budget, so make sure you won't be overspending. The most practical way to do it is to have your meal plan for a week and tick off the items needed as you buy them.

Make a List

Based on your meal plan, list all the things you'll need to buy. It saves you time instead of roaming the supermarket looking for what to buy. It will avoid impulse buying of food that you don't need, which may be wasted because you can't eat it quickly enough.

Shop with a Calculator

Use a calculator or the calculator on your phone to keep a track of what you have spent while you shop. Depending on the supermarket you may be able to scan as you shop, which will also help you to keep track. When doing your shopping, it's best to buy foods in season for a better deal. If you want fresh fruits or veggies, it usually pays to buy them from the nearest farmers' market instead of a supermarket.

To avoid spending beyond your budget, never shop for food when hungry. You are most likely to choose unhealthy foods and pick up too much.

Purchase Cold Foods and Lean Proteins

When shopping, consider ways to make delicious salads that aren't limited to romaine lettuce and standard greens. Add beans to salads to add extra protein, some dried fruit, and various vegetables.

Do you need a quick snack? Make a black bean salsa and keep it in the fridge.

Raw almonds and other nuts are a delicious way to add crunch to your meal.

Purchase instant grains to microwave and add to salads for added bulk. *Farro*, barley, and even instant brown rice work well.

What to Always Have in the Kitchen

When you have the space, maybe when you are in a flat share, you can put together a store cupboard of essential items you need to keep for cooking.

Stocking your kitchen with the following pantry essentials will make your college life more of a delightful experience than eating in the cafeteria or ordering food online.

- Onions
- Lemons
- Rice
- Oats
- Garlic
- Ginger
- Salt
- Butter
- Oil
- Vinegar
- Soy sauce
- Oyster sauce
- Sugar
- Chocolate
- Baking soda
- Honey

- Lemon
- Sesame oil
- Vegetable oil
- Ketchup
- Balsamic vinegar
- Red wine vinegar
- Chicken and beef stock
- Marinara sauce
- Canned goods (diced tomatoes, beans, fruits, etc.)
- Pure vanilla extract
- Granulated sugar
- Confectioners sugar
- Cumin
- Basil
- Rosemary
- Thyme
- Smoked paprika
- Curry
- Dried oregano
- Kosher salt
- Cinnamon
- Red pepper flakes
- Nutmeg
- Ground pepper
- Pasta and noodles
- Mayonnaise
- Milk

Other than the necessary ingredients and pantry supplies that you may need for cooking, think about the equipment that you want in the kitchen. These will include equipment such as a mini-fridge, microwave, coffee maker, Brita water filter, cutlery, dinnerware, and glasses.

Batch Cooking Weekends

Even if you've always relied on your mom's (or dad's) homemade cooking, don't be intimidated by cooking for yourself at college. Make use of cookbooks and recipes from the Internet. Watch videos to learn cooking methods.

Maybe you can get some hints, tips and even some practice with Mom or Dad before you leave home.

If you have space, you can also save time and money by cooking meals in bulk and storing them in the freezer.

Fast Meals

When you go to college you're going to need to be able to cook. Even if the dining hall is a convenient choice, it won't be available forever, and let's face it, you'll likely get bored of the food on offer. After a hard day of studying, the last thing on your mind is preparing a complete supper, but there are lots of quick and easy meals you can make.

Fast meals can be really simple! For example, the microwave can be used to make an overeasy egg. Add some avocado mash to some toast for a delicious breakfast. Add an egg to a pasta dish or a pizza for extra protein. Spread a bit of tomato puree and cheese on naan or pita bread for a quick and easy pizza.

Have a set of measuring cups in the kitchen to avoid having to use scales. When you are following a recipe use only one unit of measure, don't mix cups with ounces or grams, it will spoil the proportions.

Here are just a few meal ideas designed to be easy to put together and not damage your bank balance.

Breakfasts

The microwave oven can be used to make a *quick over-easy egg*. Have this on toast, maybe add some mashed avocado, for a delicious breakfast.

Use the fridge to make overnight oats. Use single serve bowls, small glass jars like Kilner jars or similar. You will need basic rolled oats, yogurt and fresh or frozen fruit. Put a layer of oats in the bottom of the container, as much as you want to eat. Then add a good layer of yogurt, approximately twice the depth of the oats. Add a layer of fruit. Cover with a wrap and leave in the fridge overnight. In the morning you will have a delicious breakfast. You can change this recipe up by adding honey, using granola instead of oats, or using milk instead of yogurt (put enough milk in to just cover the oats).

Make breakfast smoothies. Choose your favorite fruit, grains and vegetables to create your own smoothies. Popular options include:

Green smoothie - banana, celery, broccoli, spinach, milk and a small amount of spirulina.

Fruit and honey smoothie - banana, milk, honey, mango and other soft fruit that you have in the cupboard.

Lunches and suppers

You might like your main meal at lunch time or at the end of the day, so these recipes will work whenever you eat them.

Simple Mac n Cheese. Take half a cup of water, half a cup of macaroni, a quarter cup of milk, and a pinch of salt and mix them together in a microwave-safe bowl. Microwave for 2 - 3 minutes. Stir in a quarter cup of shredded cheese, cheddar is best and microwave for another 30 seconds. Stir and leave to rest for a minute before eating. For variety try adding chives, cooked chopped bacon, cooked sausage or spring onions.

Pesto pasta. Use a jar of pesto and some shredded cheese. Cook the pasta in a pan. Drain off the butter and stir the pesto through to taste. Add the shredded cheese and some black pepper. Re-heat for 30 seconds by stirring in the pan or microwaving if it has lost some heat and enjoy.

Simple pasta salad. This makes two servings, so you can share it or save half for the next day. Take one can of tomatoes, two servings of cooked pasta, chopped cucumber, tomatoes, canned or defrosted sweetcorn, feta cheese and a teaspoon of mixed herbs. Put the tomatoes and herbs into a pan, mix together and simmer for 10 minutes. Mix in the cooked pasta then leave to cool. When it is cool add all of the other ingredients. This is a tasty salad on its own, but you could try it with canned tuna, ham, cooked sausage - whatever you like really.

These are just a few ideas to get you started. Don't be afraid to experiment, you'll soon have a set of quick and easy meals to cook for you and your friends.

Snacks

Most college students' poor eating habits stem from a lack of thinking and preparation. Prevent this by planning your grocery purchases ahead of time. If you think you'll be studying late at night, choose some healthy snack options to satisfy your craving for crunch.

Try mixing almonds into a bag of organic microwave popcorn. It will add a little something special and keep you going late into the night—snack on dried cranberries, nuts, and a small apple during the day. Keep carrot and cucumber batons and celery ready in the fridge for snacking. The crunch satisfies cravings without the need for chips or late night fast food deliveries.

If you can't avoid eating fast food, make a good choice. Choose pizza with half the cheese, a regular-sized roast beef sandwich, a baked potato, or a green salad with low-calorie dressing. As much as possible, cut back on French fries, fried chicken, and fish sandwiches high in fat.

Vending Machines

College students also have access to vending machines in the school. However, this machine of convenience contributes to the rising levels of obesity. These vending machines provide limited healthy foods aside from being expensive.

Reconsider Your Appliances

Consider the space available to you and consider which kitchen appliances will be practical for you to use. Morning smoothies can be made with a single-serving blender. A juicing sieve can be used to make cold-pressed juice. You can make fresh almond butter for breakfast using raw almonds and coconut oil.

You can make delicious hummus with garbanzo beans to serve with pita bread or fresh vegetables. Cauliflower mash also works well. Cook your cauliflower in the microwave using a steamable package. Blend in the cheese, seasonings, and a splash of milk. It's tasty and a great way to get some extra vegetables.

Most dorm rooms have a toaster. Of course it will make delicious toast, but it would also be ideal for warming naan for open-faced pizzas or warming pitas to be filled with hummus, veggies, and feta cheese.

Study & exams

Have you ever wondered how college students like you got through their college years without putting their social life, health, academic success, and finances at risk? There are fantastic college hacks that help other college students maximize their well-being and effectiveness. They were able to have good grades and enjoy their time- and so can you if you put them to practice.

Classroom Hacks

Are you earning a bachelor's, master or doctorate? Whatever degree that may be, the following hacks can give you the success that you want:

Managing Your Schedule

If you want to have adequate time management, organize!

Think about the time you'll save if you already have your books and notes organized and if you have reminders set up for appointments and deadlines.

Here are some basic ideas to help you with getting organized, you choose which will work best for you:

Start the Semester with a Planner

Write down all assignment deadlines, activities, classes, exams, etc., to see everything at a glance and be able to think ahead.

At the start of the week or on Sunday, review your schedule so you can know what's ahead. Plan and diarize your time effectively instead of trying to remember what you need to be doing and when. Use a paper diary, electronic planner, an app on your phone - whatever works for you.

Keep your study space clutter-free and organize your textbooks and notes according to subjects. It will enable you to quickly access everything you need.

Use a Calendar and Online Management Tools

Have a look at this app – **myHomework Student Planner** – a time management app for high school and university students. It provides you with a calendar so you can track your assignments, projects, exams, and other activities. It also features a widget that lets you sync your assignments and receive reminders when they are due to avoid being caught in a deadline. This app is free, but if you want to get away with ads, you can have it for about $5 a year.

If you can, schedule your classes continuously, it will be more efficient than having them scattered the whole day. This way, you can head home earlier instead of commuting between classes.

Online classes will be another practical tip if you have a hectic semester. Online classes may require the same study time as the in-seat classes. However, you can access your modules online at your convenience to use your time more effectively.

Plan Your Weekly Schedule Every Sunday

Going through the week without a plan can be stressful and you run the risk of forgetting to do something. Taking time to plan your week ahead will provide you with enough time and space to figure out how to fit everything in and avoid the last-minute rush. Sunday is a day when you should be able to find some quiet time for planning. Do this and avoid your school days becoming frantic.

Do not skip class

It's tempting to skip classes when you don't like your professor, or the subject, or maybe you want to hang out with someone. However, remember you are there to study and reach your goals. Going to college is a significant investment. The longer you stay there, the higher the cost.

The US News declared the average cost of tuition and fees for in-state public college students is $21,629 and $35,676 for a private college (Powell et al., 2021). Remember that you and/or your parents are paying for these classes. According to Student Loan Hero, more than half of the college students in the US took out educational loans to pay for college in 2020, averaging about $29,800 in total for the time they spent in college. The average graduate paid approximately $400 monthly to pay their loan debt (Student Loan Hero, 2022). The US News and World Report further state that it takes 21 years for an average recipient to pay off their entire student loan (Bidwell, 2014).

Where to Sit

It's good that in college, you have more freedom to choose where to sit in class. But think about how your choice could affect your academic performance?

If you sit in the first few rows you will get a good view and be able to hear the class easily. You're also less likely to be distracted by students who aren't taking things as seriously as you, as people are less likely to mess around when they are close to the watchful eye of the professor!

You will get to know who the students to avoid sitting near. People who might be disruptive in their attitude to lectures, or maybe fidgety in class, on their phone etc. Just avoid the distraction of being around them.

Take Fast Lecture Notes

Taking notes is essential, you need to capture the key points of lectures so that you can refer back to them when doing further study, and for revision.

The average lecturer speaks at approximately 120-180 words per minute, which is just too fast for most people to keep up with, either in writing or typing into a device. So, writing down every word is quite impossible. However, there are hacks you can apply to take notes faster than any student.

Summarize the Lecture

The key here is to write down only the main points made and significant ideas. By summarizing the information, you are taking a more simple and organized approach than merely trying to take down everything that comes out of the lecturer's mouth.

If you attempt to take almost verbatim notes you will find that you generally won't actually take in what is being said. If you are taking summary notes you will need to listen and understand the lecture as it happens.

Summary notes are brief but to the point.

Here are summarizing tips for you.

- As the lecturer introduces a new topic, use that as a heading in your notes.
- Consider using bullet points to note the key facts and ideas under each topic.

- Use phrases and keywords that mean something to you, rather than trying to record actual sentences.
- After the lecture, immediately review your notes and expand on anything that you need to, so that you will easily remember what it all means even months or years after.

Mind Mapping

Depending on your learning style, sometimes words aren't enough to record and remember what was said at a lecture. Some people are more visual, and if you are one of them, you can try a more creative approach to note-taking through mind mapping. This tool allows you to visualize the overall structure of a specific idea.

Mind mapping also allows you to connect ideas within that particular subject, and when you can quickly highlight essential ideas. There are mind-mapping tools available online if you need help, and free videos demonstrating the technique.

Using Symbols and Abbreviations

You are already aware of the most common symbols and abbreviations you can use in your note-taking. It's a matter of integrating them into your notes to speed things up. For example,

- Numbers (#)
- Information (info)
- And (&),
- At (@)
- Weight (wt), height (ht)
- For significant notes (*)

To enhance your skill, try to learn the universal abbreviations for some commonly used words.

Another way to speed up note-taking is to drop vowels from words. Your eyes will still be able to read the words if you only used consonants, especially when you have done this for a while. This is sometimes called speed writing. (Or wrtng!).

Use a Speech-to-Text App

Using a speech-to-text app may be the quickest and easiest way to take notes. Since you are not doing any hard work but turn it on to record your professor's lecture, you are getting a massive load of information and won't be missing anything. It can be beneficial to have a transcription as a text version of your lesson to go back to if you are revising and don't understand your notes

However bear in mind that if you are revising it will take a long time to read through the whole of a long lecture. So it's worth taking brief notes at the time, then having the full transcription to refer back to when you need more explanation of a key point.

Here's a guide on how to use voice typing as a transcription tool.

- Create a new Google Doc and select [tools]
- In the toolbar, select [voice typing].
- Click the link above the [microphone icon.] It will start the recording. Once you see the microphone turn red, it means it begins transcribing.

Regardless of what approach to note-taking you prefer, there is one that works perfectly for you. Exploring the different methods is also recommended; you don't need to stick to just one strategy. You can even combine different approaches to your advantage.

Share Lecture Notes

Two heads are better than one. Most of the time, there are points that you fail to pick up when taking down notes. So, it's a great idea to find the time to share and compare notes with a classmate. They might have picked up some significant points that you overlooked.

Choosing a Major

Don't choose something because it's sensible or because people expect you to do it. Choose something you love. Choose something you can be the best at. If you choose something that you're not that interested in or don't hugely enjoy you are unlikely to take that skill in adult life working life.

Changing Your College Major

Sometimes college students need to switch their major, for many different reasons. If this happens to you, make sure you do it only once, and it's final. You won't want to spend extended years in college because you kept changing your mind. Remember that every wrong decision means additional cost, time, and effort that you wouldn't want to waste.

So, if you finally decide to change a major, here are the following steps that you must follow:

- Decide on what major to shift to.
- Review the academic requirements.
- Speak to your academic advisor about your decision.
- Submit all required documents.

Avoid Cheating and Plagiarism

There are two dishonest acts that you absolutely must not do - these are CHEATING and PLAGIARISM.

Cheating always involves the use of unauthorized sources for answering the test. It may also involve lying and taking credit for something that isn't yours. Unauthorized sources could be using concealed notes, the internet, books, or looking at your classmate's answers. School authorities decide what is authorized and unauthorized, as is stated on your college prospectus.

Plagiarism is presenting another individual's concept, idea, research, or project as your own. It's a violation of someone's intellectual rights, violating the school policy, and is also considered a criminal offense. To avoid committing this crime, which is punishable by law, you need to acknowledge and attribute the work of others by citing references or citations. Plagiarism is not limited to resources taken from a book, report, website, or journal article. It also includes those previously submitted by other students, even years before.

To avoid committing plagiarism and cheating, always think of their consequences.

To make sure you do not plagarize follow these simple rules:

- Do your work and don't pay others to do it for you.
- Present your original ideas.
- Cite all your sources when presenting ideas that are not originally yours.
- Use quotes.
- Use a plagiarism detector like Copyscape, Turnitin, or Grammarly Plagiarism checker.
- When in doubt, ask your professor.

Don't cheat:

- Avoid temptation by preparing properly for tests, exams etc.
- Keep your belongings away from you – especially your mobile phones and other devices.
- Only look at your own paper and avoid looking at other students' work.
- Don't share notes or test papers. It is also cheating when you allow someone to copy from you.

Bear in mind that if you cheat, you are depriving yourself of getting the kinds of learning that you set out to achieve. You are in college because you want to provide yourself with all the skills and tools needed for success, and cheating deprives you of having access to them.

More Tips

Early to Bed and Early to Rise

In the whirlwind of college life it might feel as if you never get time just for yourself. However, think about how it would be to have just one more hour at your disposal. How do you do this? Simple, get up an hour earlier. This is one of the most simple and powerful life hacks we can suggest to you. It will mean that you need to have a reasonable bedtime. It might mean that you struggle to get up for the first week or so. Once you have this habit though, it really can change your life.

By having an extra hour at your disposal, you can do anything you want, like eat a proper breakfast, exercise, revise or read a book, maybe go for a walk. Early morning is a peaceful lovely time of day, so enjoy it.

Get the best out of your sleep. When you have rested well during the night, you'll be able to use your time effectively, and you can participate well in your classes. You'll also be able to participate well in your classes. Your mind will become more alert than when you sleep late.

It will be easier to fall asleep if you are prepared for the next day. Pack your bag with everything you will need (notes, books, etc). If you know you have a lot on and want to make sure you don't forget everything, take just five minutes to make a to-do list. It will set your mind at ease before you go to bed.

Choosing your outfit, having your chores done, washing your hair, and preparing your meals for the next day will all mean that you can make the best of that extra hour you're giving yourself.

Limit Distractions

Learn to identify things that distract you, because they are the greatest time suckers for college students like you. Dealing with them can save you a lot of time.

If you think hanging with your peers or your roommates causes you to minimize your focus on study and take frequent timeouts, do your schoolwork in the library instead of doing it at home.

If Netflix or social media distract you, use an app like Self-Control or Clear Lock to block and limit your time on those websites.

Once you limit or eliminate time-wasting distractions, you can get your work time and use your spare time for recreation.

Ask for Someone's Help

There may be some subjects or concepts that you find difficult. Don't waste time going over and over something that just escapes you. Use your time effectively by seeking assistance, then you can move on.

Join a study group. When you discuss things with others, you will find the answers more quickly than when you try to figure them out alone.

Sift Your Extra-Curricular Activities

It's part of college life to take part in social activities. Just make sure that they won't take too much of your time to lead you astray from your personal college goals and studies.

If you are interested and want to be involved in numerous activities, remember that you will need to manage your time and probably decide that you can't actually do all of them. Ensure that each meeting or activity won't be a hustle to your studies and goals.

Sift through your priority interests and ask yourself if these interests will be valuable for your future. If you think you have a jam-packed schedule for the current semester, you can always hold off joining that group until you have a less intense schedule for the next one. Don't try to fit them all in one semester.

Try out these small tips, see the huge impact they can bring, and expect productive outcomes.

Study Hacks and Habits

College study hacks are quite different from those methods you may have used in high school, in college you need to think differently and more independently. Here are some proven study habits and hacks to help improve your access to information and memory retention, thereby improving your work and exam performance.

Where to Start with Studying

There are some very simple things you can do to set yourself up for successful study throughout your time in college. These apply to all of the different study that you will take part in, be it attending a lecture, taking part in a study group or taking part in a debate:

Show up to class - This might sound obvious, but a lot of students get very casual about lectures. Lectures are an essential part of your college learning experience. In some cases your attendance can affect your grades.

Be on time - Be on time not just for lectures but for everything. Even fellow students will get fed up if they are constantly waiting for you to turn up for things, whether social or studying.

Be polite - As the saying goes, politeness costs nothing. If you are polite people will feel relaxed and happy to be around you. However, don't confuse being polite with being a doormat - if someone is being demanding or abusing your good nature you don't have to go along with them.

Be helpful - We all like a little help sometimes. It tends to be the case that if you help others then others will help you, which can't be a bad thing. Casually offering some help when someone seems to need it can strengthen existing friendships and start new ones.

Be enthusiastic - We're not saying that you need to jump up and down and agree that everything is wonderful, that would be a bit off-putting for those around you! We're suggesting that you start by viewing the world in a positive fashion. When you are presented with a new idea, maybe that you don't agree with, don't instantly jump to squash it and put it down.

Try to start by thinking about the positive aspects and recognising them, then put your less positive view over in a balanced fashion.

Be positive - Following on from being enthusiastic - you will face challenges along the way, but try to look for the positive in every situation. If the day ahead of you looks like hard work, acknowledge that to yourself. Then think about the positives - what will you be learning during the day, which people you like will you see, and even - how great will you feel when it's over?

Find a Convenient Place to Study

It pays to be consistent when studying, so make it a habit. Find a spot where you can feel comfortable studying. Make sure it is free of distractions and conducive to studying.

This place might be in your room, but it can be depressing to spend too much time in one place. You might find a quiet corner of the library to be just the place you need.

Treasure Hunting – The Answers are Out!

Bear in mind that the questions set in college work are designed to be a rehearsal for exams. They will be in the form of tests, quizzes, homework, practice exercises, and other student resources. Bear in mind that you were provided with these exercises for a reason. Just be resourceful and don't waste any opportunity to learn from these activities.

Avoid Getting Stressed

Many students fail in examinations not because they don't know the answers, but because they get mentally blocked. Because they are more anxious about the thought of failing, what they have put in their brain was locked away somewhere that they just couldn't access when they needed to. It's hard to keep cool when you can't stop thinking about your exams, especially when you're not confident that you will pass them. Take every opportunity to practise in tests and by using sample questions from previous exams.

Discover your learning style. There are four types of learning styles.

- Auditory – learning through hearing
- Visual – learning through visuals
- Kinesthetic – hands-on learning
- Read or Write – learning through writing notes and reading textbooks and other materials.

Finding what learning style is more suitable for you can make learning more productive. Most students use a combination of these learning styles, so it pays to find out the style that works for you.

Study in Company

Two brains are better than one, and sometimes more than two brains are even better! You don't have to go through this college journey on your own. As soon as you start to get to know people who are doing the same courses as you, think about how it might be to work alongside them. Before you approach anybody to see if they would like to buddy up make sure that you consider whether you have a similar approach to them. Do they attend lectures and concentrate? Do they turn their assignments in on time? Do their comments and questions make sense to you? Do you like being around them?

These are some of the advantages of studying in company:

- First and foremost, studying with one or more people is an opportunity to practice your skills with people. This is great preparation for the world of work.
- Studying can become boring. Having company helps to keep the subject alive - you will bring different ideas and viewpoints together.

- You can help each other out with notes. If you have missed something in a lecture, or didn't quite understand the point being made, your friends can probably help you out.
- Bringing together learning from more than one person will improve your understanding and have the result that you will learn faster.
- You will help to keep each other on track. When you're studying you surely already know that it's easy to become distracted or to put off the work by doing something completely different. Study buddies set targets and help each other to keep to them.
- It can expand your horizons - members of your study group may be able to introduce you to new resources and course materials. They may be able to suggest useful study techniques that will help you to be more productive.

Organize a Study Group

Studying in company is a powerful study strategy as it combines multiple individuals' various strengths and interests. You can have a live study group, have on-line meetings or learn through a shared Google Docs folder. If you're the first one to organize this group, then you have full control of the group. You can share study docs, set up meetings, and benefit from everyone's knowledge.

A great advantage is that you have more than one person to call on if you need help. If you're working late and struggling to understand a key point, hopefully one of the study group will also be awake to pick up your text message.

Find a Study Buddy

You might prefer to work with just one person, or feel a bit daunted working in a larger group. Or you may just be lucky enough to have one individual who you work well with in addition to working in a study group. It's fantastic to find someone you really get on with who complements the way you study and learn, who can become your partner as you work through a course.

How to Make Studying With Others Work

Don't be daunted if you find yourself in a study group or pairing up with a study buddy who seems to be really on the ball with the work, or to be very clever. We all have our strengths and you might well be underestimating yourself!

People are choosing to study with you for a reason, so have confidence in yourself.

Think about the skills you bring to the situation and use them to help the dynamic. If you're an organized individual you might be the one to set up the study group meetings and on-line activities and actually make them happen. If you have a systematic and efficient way of sharing course notes, share that with your friends who make it known that they struggle with that. You might be a prolific reader who finds it easy to read additional materials and absorb them. You can share your extra learning with your fellow students.

A word of warning

Be aware that there are students who will use study groups and study buddies as a way of avoiding hard work. If you gradually realize that someone you study with isn't pulling their weight it will be a difficult situation, but you need to deal with it. If you're constantly being asked for your course notes, or to share your latest assignment, it's time to politely distance yourself from that student.

When you are studying with others you should feel that you are all taking part as equals, not giving a free ride to anyone.

Cost effective on-line materials

Always bear in mind that you are not confined to using the materials presented to you as you work through your course. Most universities and colleges provide free on-line resources for their students. Some of these are freely available to the general public. Find out what is out there that might help you.

It's also worth having a look at sources of cheap on-line learning, for example Udemy, Udacity and Skillshare. Take the time to research these to see what is applicable to your learning.

Improve Your Memory

Making good lifestyle choices – limiting stress, eating a balanced diet, getting enough sleep, and having regular mental and physical exercises is the best way to improve your memory. You could also use brain-training games to keep your mind agile.

Consider learning the following science-back strategies to improve your memory recall.

Organize Your Notes

When studying, outline information that you need to recall. You can highlight and focus on the most important ideas with an organized, detailed outline.

You can easily recall information using the chunking method that breaks down a large amount of data into smaller logical units for easy understanding. For example, learning a foreign language, you can group words into functional groups like nouns, verbs, adjectives, occupations, etc.

Make Associations

Make associations by creating mental images of things you want to recall and connecting them with sounds, tastes, colors, or tastes. For example, you want to remember a person with the surname of Barker. You can associate this person with the word bark by associating them with the bark of a tree or the sound of a dog.

Use Visual Cues

Learning can be much easier with visual tools like concept maps, graphs, photos, and illustrations. These tools simplify information, making it easier to understand and recall when needed. Visual cues are also great for boosting spatial memory as research has discovered in research among patients with Alzheimer's Disease and Mild Cognitive Impairment.

Saying It Out Loud

If you want to remember a piece of information, say it aloud. One study disclosed speaking aloud and hearing yourself will help to get information into long-term memory. The same research likewise confirms that memory benefits from active involvement (*Reading Information Aloud to Yourself Improves Memory of Materials*, 2017).

All-Nighter Tips

When things get too busy or when cramming for an exam, it's common for college students to skip a night of sleep. However, it's not safe to always fall back on all-nighters to finish your work. Health experts say that you must avoid pulling all-nighters as much as possible because of the adverse effects of sleep deprivation on your physical and mental health.

Pulling an all-nighter can leave you feeling tired, dehydrated, and with skin that looks unhealthy the next day. You may also find it hard to focus and may take up to a few days before you can catch up with your lessons. By not allowing your body to rest and recharge, your immune system can be impaired (Bologna, 2020).

It's best to sleep for a few hours instead of staying awake. Try sleeping for about 90-110 minutes to complete at least one entire sleep cycle (Yetman, 2020). Although one sleep cycle may not be sustainable, it can help restore your mind and body and get through the next day feeling less miserable.

College Activities to Try

A large part of your learning in college involves out-of-classroom activities – socialization, extra-curricular activities, community services, sports activities, etc.

Try getting involved in various groups or communities where you share the same interests.

Health

When life is too demanding for busy college students, they often let their health fall by the wayside, letting their academic activities overshadow attention to health habits – both good and bad. Good nutrition and health practices connect directly to one's physical, mental, emotional, and overall well being.

Sleep

Adults 18-60 years old need to have seven or more hours of sleep every night, while those below 18 must have 8-10 hours of sleep in 24 hours. This recommendation came from the Centers for Disease Control and Prevention (CDC) (Wallis, 2020),

Most students work hard and play hard, making time to both study and socialize. As mentioned earlier, they might pull "all nighters" or stay up very late. They are likely to have a large workload from the subjects they are taking. Added to that many students also have part-time jobs. All of this takes its toll, leaving them with low energy and motivation levels.

Students who have a lack of sleep will usually find that it is hurting their grades and health. This means that they give less attention in class, they also tend to cram before the examinations. Then they work into the night or even all night to catch up... It becomes a vicious and exhausting cycle.

Sleep deprivation can contribute to and be caused by mental health issues. Research done by the National Alliance on Mental Illness reported that 44% of students experienced symptoms of depression. About 80% feel overwhelmed by academic responsibilities, while 50% struggle with anxiety. Poor sleep likewise increases your risk of mood problems, affecting your grades and jobs.

Another significant consequence to consider is that a student who is deprived of sleep may be dangerously drowsy when driving. A lack of sleep can be hazardous and may lead to a vehicular accident. A study by the AAA Foundation for Traffic Safety divulged that you are twice more likely to get into a car accident when you only have 6-7 hours of sleep than when you have a full eight-hour quality sleep (Tefft, 2016). When your brain is tired, your response time slows down.

The negative impact of unfulfilled sleep requirements outweighs the benefits of a few hours of studying.

Benefits of Sleep

Sleep has many amazing health benefits, affecting almost every tissue in your body. It affects stress, growth hormones, immune system, breathing, appetite, cardiovascular health, and blood pressure.

Students need to sleep about eight hours to boost their physical and mental conditions. Here are some benefits you may reap from having enough quality sleep.

- Boosts immune system and heart
- Helps prevent weight gain
- Regulates mood
- Increases productivity
- Increases physical performance
- Improves memory

Use some sleep tracking apps to ensure you have a night of quality sleep. Most of these trackers are a watch that works by monitoring your body movements as you sleep. It helps you determine how much time you spent awake and the time you were asleep. Some sleep tracking devices even look at your heart rate change while asleep. These tools measure how much time you spend in each sleep cycle.

Examples of Sleep Tracking Apps are:

- SleepScore
- Sleep++
- Sleep Cycle
- PrimeNap
- Pillow

Since sleep sometimes seems like a luxury you can't afford when you are in college, developing healthy habits will help you get the benefits of good quality sleep. Relaxing your body and mind after a busy day is essential to better sleep.

Here are sleeping habits before bedtime that you can develop to help ease insomnia and transition to rest while improving overall sleep quality.

Develop a healthy sleeping pattern. Early to bed and rise is the best way to have a healthy and vibrant life during your college days. Make a habit of establishing a sleeping and waking time. Once your body's circadian rhythm gets used to your established sleeping pattern, you will find it easier to sleep and wake up on a programmed sleep schedule.

Read books before bedtime. Reading can put you in the right headspace for a good night's sleep. Reading is vital to strengthening the mind. A strong cognitive function helps lower mental chatter and lets you drop into a peaceful state of relaxation.

Stay off the Phone and Social Media. Checking your social media, reading news, or sending emails before bedtime can keep you awake. The nighttime use of electronics can affect sleep via the stimulating effects of light from the digital screen. It can interfere with your circadian rhythm – the 24-hour body clock that controls sleep-wake processes. The screen light on your device stimulates parts of your brain, making you feel more alert at bedtime when you should be winding down to relax.

Listen to music. Listening to music provides a total brain workout. A study about music has shown that listening to music has the following benefits (*Keep Your Brain Young with Music*, 2022):

- Reduces anxiety, blood pressure, and pain
- Improves sleep quality, mood, mental alertness, and memory

Some find that listening to audiobooks helps them relax and drop off to sleep.

Meditate. Do you know meditation can help you improve memory, concentration, and learning? Meditation is proven by science to enhance physical; health and mental wellbeing. It likewise reconnects you with what is present and vital in your experience.

Meditation provides you with inner peace and can help you be more successful in all your endeavors in life. It can help you to study more efficiently, improve your recall during tests, and decrease anxiety during challenging situations.

Do a Few Low-Impact Exercises. Some simple yoga positions or low-impact exercises like stretching can ease pain and aid sleep.

A review of studies revealed a link between meditative movements (such as Yoga and Tai Chi) to an improved quality of sleep, which as we've discussed before, will give a better quality of life.

Another exercise that can positively impact your sleep is stretching, which helps focus your attention on your breath and body, not stressors. Awareness of your body aids in improving mindfulness, which again will promote better sleep.

Sticking to gentle stretches before bedtime offers potential physical benefits – helping relieve muscle tension and prevent sleep-disrupting muscle cramps.

Drinks to avoid after dinner. Avoid caffeine after dinner for the reason that it will keep you awake and alert. Many people use alcohol to aid their sleep issues. However, alcohol decreases sleep quality by increasing nighttime awakenings, making your night less restful.

Nicotine in cigarettes is a stimulant. It can keep you awake. It can also cause problems waking up and also brings you nightmares. If you are smoking, try not to smoke two hours before bedtime.

If you want a hot drink in the evening, milky drinks will help you to relax and fall asleep.

Naps

An after-lunch nap can help boost your dwindling energy levels, but don't nap for longer than an hour and never later than 2:00 to 3:00 p.m.

Sleep Problems

If you have sleep issues like insomnia even after following our tips, consider checking up with the school physician. You may have sleep problems because of an underlying issue. Common conditions often associated with sleep issues include (*How to Keep a Mental Health Journal*, 2022):

- Mental health issues
- Diabetes
- Musculoskeletal disorders
- Kidney disease
- Neurological disorders
- Thyroid disease
- Respiratory problems
- Heartburn
- Heart attack & heart failure
- Diabetes
- Blood pressure
- Stroke

Water

Benefits of Drinking Water

Water is your body's principal chemical component and makes up about 55% to 60% of your body (Water Science School, 2019). Water is one of the bare essentials in life that we all depend on for survival. All parts in our bodies - cells, tissues, and organs need water to work correctly. Waters keeps every system in your body functioning properly.

The Harvard TH Chan School of Public Health claims that water performs many essential functions (*The Importance of Hydration*, 2018):

- Aiding your digestion
- Lubricating and cushioning joints
- Transporting nutrients and oxygen to all cells across the body
- Flushing harmful organisms from your bladder
- Preventing constipation
- Regulating body temperature

- Protecting body tissues and organs
- Maintaining electrolyte or sodium balance in your body
- Regulating blood pressure

You risk dehydrating if you do not drink enough daily.

The U.S. National Academies of Sciences, Engineering, and Medicine suggested that an adequate fluid intake for women is about 11.5 cups or 2.7 liters a day. Such recommendations include water, beverages, and fluids from food. Only twenty percent of your daily fluid intake comes from food and eighty percent from drinks.

Dehydration warning signs could be:

- Confusion
- Dizziness
- Weakness or low energy
- Low blood pressure
- Dark-colored urine

Can you drink too much water if you have certain health conditions like kidney, liver, or heart disease? If you have significant health issues check with your doctor.

If you take medication that causes you to sweat more, such as nonsteroidal anti-inflammatory drugs (NSAIDs), opiate pain medications, or some antidepressants, drinking more water can work to your advantage, check this with your doctor.

Remember that it's not only water that can keep you hydrated. Beverages also contribute to your daily requirement for fluids. Avoid sugary drinks as they can cause inflammation (Harvard Health, 2021). You can also try some herbal teas. You might try ginseng tea for energy and chamomile tea for relaxation.

The best way to consume water is to drink it throughout the day and at each meal. Bear in mind that you need to drink more water before, during, and after workouts, at high altitudes, when you have a fever, and during hot and humid weather.

To check if you're drinking enough, you should rarely feel thirsty, and the color of your urine should be pale yellow to colorless.

Eyesight

As a student, take care of your eyes because they will be working as hard as you. Eye issues can develop without signs or symptoms so make sure that you get regular checkups with an optician. If you wear contact lenses, consider leaving them out for a day if your eyes are tired and dry. Always remove your eye makeup before going to bed.

Several studies indicate that digital devices are harmful to human health. Eighty-eight percent of Americans know that digital devices can adversely affect their vision, but they still spend seven or more hours per day in front of their screens (van Hise, 2017).

The average millennial spends nine hours daily on devices such as smartphones, tablets, LED monitors, and flat-screen TVs.

As a student you won't be able to avoid spending long hours using screens. Make sure that your workstation is set up properly and take regular breaks away from the screen. Even if you just raise your eyes from the screen every twenty minutes and focus on a corner of your room it will help.

Approximately 11 million Americans beyond 12 years old need vision correction (*Keep an Eye on Your Vision Health*, 2020).

Common causes include:

- Too much time spent on screens
- Glare from computer screens
- Reading and studying with poor lighting
- Lack of eye blinking
- Not enough sleep
- Poor sitting posture
- Too close to the computer screen
- Uncorrected vision issues
- Poor diet
- Sharing makeup
- Inadequate hygiene measures like rubbing eyes, infrequent hand washing
- Swimming or showering in contact lenses

To reduce eye strain, we suggest that you:

- Position your desktop monitor roughly an arm's length away from your eyes to minimize any distracting screen reflections - e.g., windows or any shiny objects.

- Give your eyes a restful break by looking at something 20 feet away for about 20 seconds. Do this every 20 minutes.
- Blink regularly. Focusing your eyesight on the screen makes you blink less, which causes your eyes to dry and become uncomfortable.
- Use protective glasses, such as blue light prevention glasses, when working on screen.

Posture

Rounded shoulders are usually caused by muscle imbalances, poor posture habits, and excessive focus on specific exercises.

Nevertheless, having rounded shoulders can be alleviated. When your muscles and joints are used to hunch forwards, they can be retrained to find the proper resting position.

To correct your bad posture, you must be aware of everyday habits that may affect your sitting, lying, or standing. Sometimes, treating this issue is very simple. Because college students spend much time sitting inside the classroom or in the dormitory studying, many suffer from symptoms including upper back pain and stiffness, muscle spasms, headache, localized shoulder pain, and trap pain because of bad posture. Here are tips to prevent these and avoid back issues later in life.

- Consider your chair and how you sit.
- Review the position of how you look at your cell phone or desktop computer
- Make sure you have a good mattress
- If you wake up with neck pain, try a different or remedial pillow
- Walk and listen to audio
- Consider learning Pilates exercises, Yoga, the Alexander Technique or at least taking part in active sports.

Toothache

It is crucial to look after your teeth, especially when you're away from home. A little care and attention can avoid any toothache and other teeth issues. Brush and floss your teeth regularly after every meal. As much as possible, avoid sugary foods, drinks and sweets that generate acid in the mouth that may cause problems. In case of gum issues such as ulcers, gargle with salt water. Have a checkup with the dentist twice a year.

Skincare

Because we are constantly exposed to various pollutants in our environments, it is a must to cleanse your skin regularly, whether you wear makeup or not. Here is a skincare routine to ensure that you maintain fresh-looking and vibrant skin regardless of how busy you are.

After hopping out of bed, cleanse your face with lukewarm water and facial soap or wash to remove excess oil and dead skins.

When you shower, cleanse your whole body and use skin exfoliating body salt from time to time to remove dead skin cells. This will leave your skin feeling happy and refreshed. Also, don't forget to wear flip-flops in communal showers to avoid verrucas.

In the morning, take Vitamin C and apply SPF lotion before going out to protect your skin from the harmful ultraviolet rays. In the evening, you might use a retinol. Retinol exfoliates and brightens skin tone. It also improves your skin's firmness and elasticity.

Colds, Coughs, and Being Sick

While no specific food can cure an illness, eating the right foods can help relieve symptoms and discomfort, making you feel better. Here are some of the foods to eat when you're sick.

Fresh Fruits

When you have cold and flu symptoms, make sure that you have a stock of fresh fruits. They are full of vitamins, minerals, and other nutrients that can help boost your immune system. You may choose to eat various fruits, but citrus fruits like lemon, oranges, and grapefruits are rich in Vitamin C, which can help strengthen your immune system and fight colds and flu.

Herbal Teas

Even when you're not sick, herbal teas are good for your body because of their many health benefits. They are a great idea when you have colds and flu as they help relieve symptoms of sore throat and upset stomach and keep you hydrated. Ginger and green tea have sound anti-inflammatory effects. Mint and chamomile teas are great to soothe an upset stomach. Turmeric teas are thought to have healing properties. You could add honey to your tea if you can't drink unsweetened tea, as honey is soothing when you have a cold.

Soup

A bowl of hot chicken soup is great for making you feel warm and relaxed and for relieving fever and other cold symptoms.

First-Aid Tips

Since you will be living far from home, having a first-aid kit is a must. Anything can happen anytime; the best thing you can do is be ready.

First-Aid Equipment

- Digital thermometer
- Medical gloves
- Instant ice packs
- Disposable masks
- Hand sanitizer
- Medical scissors
- Hydrogen Peroxide
- Adhesive bandages
- Disposable masks
- Antiseptic wipes
- Cotton balls

Medications

For Wounds and Sunburns:

- Sunburn relief cream or spray
- Antiseptic ointment

For Aches and Pains

- Ibuprofen
- Paracetamol or acetaminophen
- Kerouac

For Colds and Coughs

- Fever relievers
- Nasal spray and decongestants
- Cough and colds medications

For Allergy

- Anti-itch creams
- Antihistamine tablets

For Digestive Disorders

- Antacid
- Antidiarrheal medications

Menstruation

Don't forget to take care of yourself during your period. For some it's not a particularly difficult time but many suffer from painful dysmenorrhea, bloating and possibly migraines. You're used to this when you were at home of course, but probably you had support from your family. Now you need to remember to take care of yourself.

It might be helpful to keep a menstrual diary. This will help you to make sure that you have the physical things you need at the ready. It will also remind you to be ready to take migraine medication at the first sign of trouble.

Have painkillers ready in case you will need them. Avoid caffeine and sugar when you have cramps, they can make them worse.

If you need to stop and rest, go home and do just that. Sleep if you need to, stay hydrated, avoid screen use. Keep warm and hug a heat pack or hot water bottle if it helps. You know your own body. If you develop any new or worrying symptoms consult a doctor.

Exercise

When you're really busy doing all that college stuff, you might think that fitness in college is unrealistic. Of course, it's not true! If anything you need to be even stronger and fitter to keep up with your workload. Regular working out is good for you.

Exercise is commonly known as the best way to get physically strong, but a new study shows that it can also make you mentally stronger by making you feel better.

New research published in the Journal of Happiness Studies shows that even 10 minutes a week of physical activity can make you much more likely to feel happy (Zhang, 2018).

Countless studies have linked physical exercise and happiness. Researchers found that people who worked out for at least 30 minutes several days a week were about 30% more likely to say they were happy than those who worked out for less time. They also found that getting more exercise can make you much less likely to become depressed (Mejia, 2018).

There's still much to be done to find out if there is an ideal amount of exercise to make people happier. It's thought that physical activity could be used to prevent or treat mental disorders, it will be interesting to see if research is carried out in the future on that. It's clear that there is a link between physical activity and mental wellbeing.

Many of the most influential people today, like Richard Branson, Mark Zuckerberg, Oprah Winfrey, and Mark Cuban, say that being physically active has helped them become successful and happy.

In her book "Time Smart," Harvard professor Ashley Whillans said that putting more value on time than money will make you happier and improve your quality of life. In an interview, she claimed that research repeatedly shows that people who put time first are happier than people who put money first. It is partly because putting time first makes us feel we have more control over our everyday lives. She says you should fill your days with "time-abundant activities," or ones that are important to you.

When you are studying hard, it can be difficult to find time for other activities. Whillans coined the term "happiness dollars" to show how happier certain things can make you. Let's say you get a $10,000 raise, for example. It's suggested that a raise of $10,000 will make you happier by a certain amount, so that amount is the happiness dollar value of the raise. However, you can do other things that will make you just as happy. Doing a form of exercise that you enjoy might also have a value of happiness is also $10,000.

Whillans suggested that, for example, getting help with chores can make you $18,000 happier. Just think of that when you and your roommate are tidying up!. She also said that you could be $1,800 happier if you spent 30 minutes a day on what she calls "active leisure." It could be anything from working out to helping others.

Cardio and aerobic Exercises

Exercise can help you do better in school. During exam season, it's easy to put your health and fitness at the bottom of your list of things to do. But do you know that exercise has a lot of benefits that will help you with your schoolwork?

Think about these reasons why you should try to get some exercise every day:

Higher Levels of Energy

Experts have found a link between being physically healthy and doing well in school. It is because low-intensity exercise can give us a much-needed boost of energy, which is excellent when you have to study for a long time. Studies also show that exercise makes people more creative and gives them more mental energy. So, if you need ideas, a walk or jog might be all it takes to develop something extraordinary.

Better Memory

Research shows that when you work out, your brain releases proteins that can help improve your memory and make you smarter. This is because those proteins have a significant effect on the hippocampus, a part of the brain that helps us remember things. So, regardless of whether you're studying for an exam or listening to a lecture, you'll find it much easier to understand and remember what you learn if you work out regularly.

Better Concentration

Blood flows to the brain when you do anything that makes you work out hard. It makes your neurons fire up and helps cells grow, especially in the hippocampus. It also means that if you work out for just 20 minutes before your study time, you can improve your ability to focus and pay attention.

Improved mood

Doing some physical activity makes your brain and spinal cord produce more endorphins. Endorphins are famous "feel good" chemicals produced by your body. Endorphins will also make you feel less stressed, improving your brain's function in several ways. So, if you start to feel like you have too much on your plate, regular exercise will help to keep stress at bay and help you maintain a positive attitude.

Now that you know that exercise helps your brain in many ways, why not go for a walk, jog, or run?

10,000 Daily Steps

You may have heard that walking 10,000 steps a day is good for you, but do you know why?

In the last ten years, the number of people who track their steps has exploded. People run to see how fit they are or to compete with their friends. The current advice is to take 10,000 steps every day - but why?

Even though this "recommendation" wasn't based on science initially, science shows that 10,000 steps a day are a great goal.

If 10,000 steps seem like a lot, there's good news. You can start with less and still benefit more from walking. Managing only half of that amount is linked to a lower chance of dying young. It doesn't mean that getting more than 5,000 steps isn't better, but even a little more movement each week is good for you.

Research shows that the more active you are every day, even if it's just light activity, the better. Many American adults find walking 10,000 steps a day hard, but it is possible (Upham, 2019).

Health Benefits of Light Activities

Surprisingly, even small changes in how much you move during the day can have significant effects. A recent study showed that the risk of dying early drops by 17% if you don't sit for 30 minutes daily. It includes walking, yoga, skipping, stretching, etc. Exercise with higher intensity, of course, has more benefits and reduces the risk by 35%.

How to Get Started

If you have never tried tracking your steps before, start by keeping track of your regular daily steps for a week or two. Then give yourself a goal to move more than you usually do.

The most important thing about keeping track of your regular steps is to be mentally prepared for days when you don't reach your goal and days when you go above and beyond it. Getting to 10,000 steps can be a good goal, but if you get down on yourself when you miss that target, you might want to re-evaluate. Just go outside and move around more than you did yesterday.

What Does the Number Signify?

The idea that 10,000 is a magic number came from a Japanese marketing campaign in 1965. A Japanese health science professor had invented a pedometer and thought that if people walked 10,000 steps a day, they wouldn't get fat. The pedometer was called "Manpo-Kei," which means "10,000-step meter." Since then, the advice to take 10,000 steps has stuck, but obviously there are no guarantees that you won't get fat!

Getting Into Sports

College girls indulging in sports have higher levels of self-esteem and confidence. They also have a lower risk of depression. There could be a number of reasons for this, being part of a team is likely to boost self-esteem and confidence for example, but taking part in sport is generally good for wellbeing.

Mental Health

While you often concentrate on your academic performance, you overlook your mental health. A research study suggested that 50% of mental health issues are established by age 14 and 75% by 24 (Mental Health Organization, 2016).

There are many ways to consider improving your health.

Mindfulness

Mindfulness is an approach to mental wellbeing that focuses on being aware of our feelings, thoughts, environment and even our bodily sensations. This should be done in a nurturing and gentle state of mind. Mindfulness helps us to live in the present rather than dwelling on the past and re-hashing negative experiences or worrying about the future. It has a calming effect and uses techniques including guided imagery and different relaxation and breathing exercises to soothe your body and mind.

Mindfulness can help college students to cope with the many pressures of college by teaching them to focus on things that matter most. It creates awareness while assisting them in mastering their emotions and dealing more productively with their workloads.

Meditation

One of the most effective approaches to practicing mindfulness is meditation. It is about soothing your mind and senses, achieving calmness, and reaching a state of tranquility.

Meditation involves practicing deep breathing, focusing on a certain point in space or your mind, and chanting a mantra. You can find free meditation videos on-line where a speaker will talk you through guided meditation.

Journaling

Another way to cope with stress, anxiety, and depression in college is through journaling. You can also use journaling to improve your behavior and habits.

When you are ready to start journaling, pick a convenient time to write every day about anything you find significant that happens during that particular day. You may spend 10-15 minutes doing this. Writing your journal can help you process your emotions and work on your self-improvement goals.

To start the journal habit, follow these steps.

Decide if you want to use pen and paper or a digital journal tool.

- Assign a convenient time for you to write in your journal. Could it be before bedtime, after your lunch break, or as soon as you arrive home in the afternoon? You may not necessarily do it daily. You can do it if you only have the time or during weekends.
- When you write, don't worry about your grammar or vocabulary. Just concentrate on your thoughts and emotions. Remember that you are doing this to express yourself so you can find a way to improve yourself.
- If you're having a tough time, think about whether you are still able to record at least one positive thing that happened during the day. It might be as simple as enjoying your lunch or exchanging a few words with another student.

Put anything you like in your journal and use any format you like. Some write their journal as a letter, others as a novel or a list. Include things that interest you or make you reflect:

- Poem or song lyrics
- Anecdotes and jokes
- Quotes that catch your attention
- Drawings or images

Use your journal for reflection and as a reminder of the things in life you need to deal with. Some examples might be:

- Feelings of depression or loneliness.
- Spending more time doing something you enjoy.
- Getting a medical opinion on something that's bothering you, for example a mole that needs checking out.
- The people in your life. Are there some you would like to spend more time with? Are there others who bring you down that you might want to drift away from?
- Anything that regularly causes you stress and plan how to deal with it.
- Obstacles to your studies and how to overcome them.

Technology Hacks

Let's think about how you can look after the technology in your life, so that everything is working efficiently and is properly cared for.

You'll want to get the best out of your devices and one of the most simple ways to do this is to maximize the efficiency of battery use. These tips will help to extend the working life of your batteries and generally care for your devices so that they run as efficiently as possible.

- Turn down the light - Reduce screen brightness. If it is available on your device make sure that adaptive brightness is turned on. This means that the device will automatically adjust brightness depending on the light in the room.
- Reduce notifications - Consider turning off push notifications and only checking messages periodically. This will also reduce distractions. If you still want to use push mail make sure that they are only turned on from the apps you are interested in.
- Reduce the "timeout" period. Set the time for your screen to close after not being used to say two or three minutes.

- Keep your operating system up to date, either by allowing auto downloads or by checking regularly to see if there are downloads waiting. This will mean that you benefit from updates that improve the efficiency of your devices as soon as possible.
- You could consider turning off wireless features such as Bluetooth and Near-Field Communication (NFC) to save battery life. If you do this just be aware that some of your favorite apps might need them to keep working correctly. For example, NFC is used for mobile payments by Apple and Google. If you have limits on your data plan you will want to use wifi when you're at home.
- Use Power Saver Mode - If you're using a device and are worried that the battery is going to run out, switch to Power Saver Mode. Most devices do this automatically when the battery gets very low, but there is nothing to stop you doing it sooner. It will affect the screen display and may turn off some features, but could be useful if you're working away from a power supply.
- Beware of apps that use a lot of power - playing games, watching films, surfing the Internet, playing music - these will all drain your battery down.
- Carry a battery pack - Keep a fully charged battery pack (or power bank) with you so that you can charge up when there are no electric sockets available.

- Care for your tech - Keep your devices dry and cool. For example if you're going to the beach, cover your phone and keep it out of direct sunlight. Make sure that the vents for your laptop fan are clean. Be aware that placing it on a soft surface such as your bed might block the vents and cause it to overheat.
- Eating and drinking - Crumbs don't help keyboards. Spilled drinks kill laptops. Think about what you have around your devices.

Caring For Your Computer

Take care of your laptop or computer because it's going to work hard for you.

- Clean the keyboard regularly using a soft brush or cotton swab between the keys and appropriate cleaning spray on a soft cloth. (Not sprayed directly onto the keyboard). You can turn your keyboard or laptop upside down and tap it gently to remove crumbs and other debris, but don't shake it! Spray cans of air for removing dust are great for cleaning keyboards.
- Clean the screen regularly with screen wipes.
- As in the previous section, pay attention to your battery use, close apps that are not in use, consider screen saver timing and energy saver options available.
- If you have to spend a long period of time working without access to power, put your laptop into Airplane Mode to extend the battery life.
- Consider having a spare battery for your laptop.

- Keep drinks well away from your computer. You might think you'll never accidentally knock your juice into your computer... until you do!
- Backup your data. Make sure that all your work is automatically being stored in the Cloud, or if you don't trust the Cloud an external device. Think about how much work you can do when you're busy, even in just thirty minutes. You would not want to lose it in a computer crash.

Google Chrome

Ways to Use Google in Searching Information

Google search is used every day by millions of people for a wide range of reasons. Students use it for school activities, people in business use it for research, and many others use it for fun. However most people may not be getting the most out of Google Search.

Want to use Google search more effectively and quickly find what you're looking for? Listed below are 11 tips and tricks to help you get the most out of your Google search:

Google tabs. Use the tabs in Google search. You can find multiple tabs at the top of every search. Most of the time, there will be web, images, news, and more. Using these tabs, you can tell what kind of search you need to do. Use the News tab to find the most recent news stories. You can also search by an image by dragging an image into the image section.

Detailed search hack #1 - Use quotes. Use quotes when looking for something specific to make Google search on point as much as possible. When you enclose your search parameters in quotes, you tell the search engine to look for the whole phrase.

If you search for Puppy Dog Sweaters without quotes, the engine will look for content with those three words in any order.

But searching for "Puppy Dog Sweaters" will only look for that exact phrase. It can help you find specific information that might be buried under other content if it isn't organized well.

Detailed search hack #2 - Use a hyphen to leave out words. You might sometimes be looking for a word with more than one meaning. Mustang is one such car. When you type "Mustang" into Google, you might get results for both the Ford car and the horse. If you want to filter one, use a hyphen to tell the engine not to look at the other.

Typing "Mustang-cars" tells the search engine to look for mustangs but to get rid of any results that include the word "car." It can be helpful when you want to find out about something without learning about something else.

Sites that are like other sites. Let's say you have a website you like to visit, but it is starting to get boring, and you want to find more like it. It is a trick you can use.

By typing "related:amazon.com," you will find links to online stores like Amazon. Online stores like Barnes & Noble, Best Buy, and others sell physical goods. It's a powerful Google search tool that can help you find new sites to look at.

Math with Google Search. Google Search can help you with math. You can ask Google basic questions or some more difficult ones. It's important to remember that Google won't solve all math problems but will solve a good number of them.

In the Google search bar type in: 5*5=

Then google will show you the answer.

Look for more than one word at once. Google search is easy to change. It knows that you might not find what you're looking for if you only search for one word or phrase. So, it lets you look for more than one.

You can search for one word or phrase along with another word or phrase by using this trick. It can help you narrow your search to find what you want.t

You can find both phrases by typing "How to Prepare for a Job Interview the Best Way" OR "What to Do to Get Ready for a Job Interview." Although the parameter is the same as the quotes, only these two phrases will be searched for.

It can also be done with words, for example, by typing "white chocolate OR chocolate" without the quotes. It will look for pages that have either chocolate or white chocolate!

Shortcuts on Google Search. You can type in many commands that will give you results right away.

Like the math example above, Google can immediately give you the necessary information. It will be at the top of the search results. It can save you time and effort by keeping you from having to click on many annoying links.

Here are some of what you can tell Google to do:

- Weather *zip code* – This will tell you what the weather is like in the given zip code. You can also use the names of towns and cities instead of area codes, but this may not be as accurate if the city has more than one area code.

- What is (name of celebrity) 's Number? It is a fun little thing that will tell you how many connections any celebrity has to the famous actor Kevin Bacon. Six Degrees joke of Kevin Bacon is a popular joke that says no actor is more than six links away from Kevin Bacon. The Bacon Number for Mark Zuckerberg is 3.

Another example of math is the one shown above.

- What does the word "word" mean? Or Define *word*: This will show you what a word means.
- Time *place*: If you type in a location, this will show the time there.

You can check any stock by going to Google and typing in its ticker name. If you search for GOOG, the stock prices for Google will be checked.

With these quick commands, a web search that usually takes several clicks can be done in just one. It is beneficial if you need the same information over and over.

Specific file types. People often forget that Google search lets you look for a particular file or type. It can be very useful if you need to find a PDF or PowerPoint file you saw before or used for another project. It's easy to understand:

filetype:pdf *Search term here*

In the example above, you must change the search term to whatever you're looking for. Then, use the filetype command and enter the extension for any file type you can think of.

It is primarily useful for academic purposes but can also be helpful for business and other types of presentations.

Changes in money and units. When searching via Google, you can quickly and accurately convert both units of measure and the value of a currency. You may use it for many things, such as checking the exchange rate between two currencies. If you are learning math, you can use it to change feet to meters or ounces to liters. Here's what you need to do:

Miles to km: This will change miles to kilometers. You can change a number by putting a number in front of it. Like, "10 miles to km" will tell you how many kilometers are in 10 miles.

US Dollars to British Pounds: This turns one US dollar into one British pound. Like the measurements above, you can add numbers to find exact conversions for a certain amount of money.

This tip is indeed for math students and people who do business worldwide. But you'd be surprised at how often regular people use these tips.

Follow up on your Packages. The last thing you can do to find your packages is to use Google. You can put the tracking number for any UPS, USPS, or FedEx package right into the Google search bar, which will show you where your package is.

It's much easier to do this than to go to each site, wait for it to load, and then look for your packages. Just type in your package's tracking number to find out where it is.

Google Search is a very effective way to find information. You can find anything you need on the World Wide Web using the tips above. There is a way to make it work for you, whether you need to avoid Wikipedia for a school essay project, find the latest stock prices, or look up song lyrics.

Creating Folders on the Google Chrome Top Bar

To make a folder: If you have multiple bookmarks on the same subject on your Chrome browser, you might want to make a folder to keep them all in one place. First let's make a few folders on your google chrome top bar. I would suggest you start with these folders College, Trips, Family, Social media, etc. Here is how you make a folder on Google Chrome.

Right click on your Google Chrome browser.

Click ADD FOLDER.

Name your new folder and click SAVE.

Then you bookmark a webpage (maybe it's a trip you're planning, or an online study resource you need for college), it will appear on the google chrome top bar. Drag this name to one of the new folders you created.

Money

You're young, you're free and you're at college. It may feel like the world's your oyster, but of course there are limits. One of those is that you will need money to get out and socialize, go to gigs and generally have fun. To make sure you make the best of your money, so that you have enough for essentials as well as some treats, you will need to learn to manage your finances.

Being at college you have a great opportunity to develop good money management. This will help you to avoid financial stress and also help you to develop habits that will help you for the rest of your life.

You should use this time to calculate exactly how much money you need on a weekly basis as you go through college. Then you will know how much money you will have available to start saving. Doing this will mean that you can start to think about future goals, such as traveling, paying off your student loan and other milestones such as finding your own place when you leave college.

Managing Your Money

Let's think about some key skills that you will need to develop to manage your money. These will include setting a budget, monitoring your expenditure, saving and managing debt. These skills are as important as the skills you will be developing to support you in your studies. Also if you feel confident about your money management you will not be worried about making ends meet, or distracted from your studies by that worry.

Aim to embark on college life in good financial shape and be in the same great situation when you graduate.

Budgeting and tracking expenses

Mapping your budget and setting your financial goals may seem overwhelming after having a long day of class activities, lessons, etc. (not to mention your other obligations outside school). However, setting up a budget plan could also be not as tough as you think.

You will need to consider three significant budgeting elements:

- Earnings
- Expenses
- Savings

Tracking all these three, either manually or using a budget app, will help you manage your monthly budget.

Creating your monthly budget plan and tracking your habitual spending will give you an insight into where your money goes. You will be able to see if you set your budget correctly and if not, re-assess the plan. Be prepared to cut back if you find you are spending too much on any area, but don't set a plan that is too tough to stick to. You are allowed to have some treats and you will deserve a break from your college work.

Now, think about everything that needs to be paid monthly or prioritized, such as:

- Basic college expenses like tuition, room, and board (if you are living outside campus)
- Textbooks and class supplies
- Car insurance and payments or transportation costs
- Haircut

- Toiletries
- Food
- Phone

Use a spreadsheet or use a budget planning tool or app to set up your budget plan. Enter each of your items of expenditure into the plan with a realistic estimate of what it will cost each month. Total it up and you will know if your spending plans are realistic and manageable.

Set up another spreadsheet to use for recording what you actually spend during the month. Note how much you spent and what it was spent on. This may seem like a tiresome exercise, and it would be easy to forget to do it. However if you take the time it will be really useful to be able to compare this to your original budget plan to make sure that your original estimates were on track.

There are tracking apps, such as Wall, Acorn or Mint, that you can use to make monitoring your budget easy.

What will you do with any money left over? The sensible thing would be to save it for unexpected expenses in the future. We're sure that sometimes you'll instead use it for a fun night out with friends!

Savings

Many people struggle to save. It's so easy to just spend all of our money and forget about the future. If you can set up good saving habits when you are young then saving becomes easy. It is usually something that people will continue to do for the rest of their lives.

The easiest way to save is to include an amount to be saved each month in your budget plan. Then, rather than transferring money each month, set up a standing order for the money to be moved automatically each month. After a few months you will almost forget that it's happening.

A savings pot will be a great help when unexpected expenses come up. Maybe you'll need a particular book, or your laptop will need repairing, or there will be a field trip you want to go on. Having savings will help you to avoid using credit for these expenses.

Your savings will be your emergency fund, something everyone would like to have.

How to keep expenses down

Plan Your Meals. As we've mentioned earlier in this book, planning your meals so that you can avoid impulse buying in the supermarket is a great way to control spending. Avoid pricey takeouts or eating out. If you and your roomie get on well you might be able to meal plan and shop together, which could save even more.

Save on textbooks and devices. Rather than purchasing new editions, rent or buy old textbooks. Other, less expensive coursework resources may be available through your college.

If you need new technology for class, consider buying a refurbished model rather than a new one.

Instead of spending much on fuel, insurance, and parking space fees throughout your college years, why not consider walking, riding your bike, or taking public transportation?

Budgeting and saving, like so many other aspects of life, require time and experience to master. Don't be concerned if you occasionally make errors or go over budget. Just tweak your budget plan and get back on track. Maintain your focus on developing sound financial habits and you won't regret it.

Making Money

Even while you are in college, there are many ways you can make money. You can work part-time, have summer jobs, or work online as a freelancer. Online platforms offer various gigs and side hustles, allowing you to work during the available time. Here are some of them.

- Upwork
- Freelancer
- Fiverr
- TopTotal

There are unlimited ways to earn money physically or virtually. It's just a matter of finding what is best for you and tapping into these resources.

Gaining job experience now will help you after college when seeking employment. You will start to learn about the world of work. Earning your own money will help to boost your confidence and self-esteem and give you more independence. You might be able to pay money towards your tuition, meaning that you will need to borrow less in the future.

When you start job hunting you could consider looking for opportunities to use skills that you already have. On the other hand, it could be an opportunity to be trained in something completely new.

If you only want to work during the summer, make the most of your summer employment. Consider taking on additional shifts to make extra money to save. You might also consider doing an internship, which would provide you with both money and real-world experience if it is paid.

Success does not happen overnight, so if the going is a bit tough at first don't give up. Earning money during your time at college can mean that your life is a bit more comfortable there. It may mean that you have some cash in hand after graduation. It might even give you a healthy bank balance to give you a solid financial foundation for your future.

Avoiding Debt

Credit cards can provide convenient access to items for things you need, but also those you don't need. They are a temptation to spend money even when you don't have any. To buy that nice item of clothing or tech gadget now, rather than in a few weeks when you've saved up. In short, credit cards are a great way to drown yourself in debt quickly.

Avoid getting yourself into debt. This may seem obvious now but you might need to keep reminding yourself when you are in college. Think of ways to support yourself financially so that you don't feel so tempted. We've talked about working in college, you could also consider applying for scholarships and grants. Every college and university makes grants, with the number one eligibility requirement being high school grades.

Student Loans

Student loans have become a serious issue for students, not only in the United States. US Student loan totals have reached over $1.73 trillion (Hess, 2021). UK graduates have the highest student loan debt in the developed world. The average student will accrue over 50,000 pounds of debt before graduation (University of the People, 2022).

With such statistics, the best way to avoid debt is by earning income and paying for your education, with or without your parents' support. If this may sound impossible in your case, paying for a part of your loan while still in college can make a huge difference. The sooner you can earn money to finance your schooling, the less dependent you are on an educational loan.

If you intend to apply for a student loan, try not to take a loan amount higher than your expected first year's salary. It's best to choose federal loans over private loans because the government offers fixed interest rates. Also, learn about the deferment period to determine when you should pay back or if there is a chance for loan forgiveness.

Plan Ahead for Debt Pay Off

Two out of every three 2018 graduates had student debt, according to The Institute for College Access and Success. After your grace period expires you'll have to repay your student loans. Going from paying nothing to hundreds of dollars per month may seem surreal. You may design a long-term debt payoff plan that sets you in a good position once you graduate if you consider your total expected debt, repayment schedules, and interest.

If you've accumulated a lot of student loans, personal loans, or credit card debt you'll need a strategy to repay them.

It would be best to confront your debt head-on as soon as possible to build a stable financial future. You can pay off the debt using different methods, but the one that keeps you motivated is the best option. For example, set your monthly payment plan with some small rewards along the way. Plan that when you have paid the first 12 months of payments without missing a month you can get yourself a reward, maybe a concert ticket or an item of clothing you'll love.

Start Investing

The earlier you invest, the longer the time your money will earn interest and the more money will be in your pot for when you need it. Think about setting up a personal pension plan as soon as you start work, the earlier you start the larger your pension will be.

Investing is much easier than you would believe. You can start an account online with a little deposit and set up automatic monthly transfers to your investing account from your bank account. If you're considering starting an Individual Retirement Account or investing in the S&P 500 or similar, do your homework beforehand and consider getting independent financial advice.

Test Out Financial Planning Apps and Resources

Aside from your bank's app, there's much more to managing money on your phone. Nowadays, budgeting services such as Mint and You Need a Budget can help you organize your finances in ways that make saving easier.

Experiment with a few to see how they perform. They may not be the ones you want to use in the long run, but knowing how each program works will help you sort through various money management approaches to discover the one that's right for you.

Your work is never done when it comes to financial literacy. Like everything else in life, the money world is constantly changing and rebranding.

You may believe that the tools and knowledge you've acquired are ample at this time, but you never know what financial problems and opportunities lie ahead of you.

Search for and follow a reputable media outlet (such as Forbes, Bloomberg, The Balance, or The Motley Fool) on social media platforms or subscribe to their newsletters if you trust their advice.

Finally

What more can we say? We hope that this book has given you some help and ideas as you prepare for this next huge and exciting step in your life. From living away from home to managing your money, from keeping healthy to the world of dating, we've tried to share the things that we wish we'd been told before we embarked on college life.

Please don't be daunted by the prospect of going to college. Yes, it might be a bit challenging at times, you might feel out of your depth at first, but you've got this! Your time at college is going to be amazing. You will meet fascinating people and make great friends, some of whom will be friends for life. You will go into college as a child and leave an adult ready to make your way in the world. And your college days will be the best days of your life.

Enjoy the journey!

References

Bidwell, A. (2014, October 7). *Student Loan Expectations: Myth vs. Reality.* US News. https://www.usnews.com/news/blogs/data-mine/2014/10/07/student-loan-expectations-myth-vs-reality

Bologna, C. (2020, February 20). *The Scary Ways An All-Nighter Messes With Your Body And Brain.* HuffPost. https://www.huffpost.com/entry/what-happens-when-you-pull-an-all-nighter_l_5dd5b559e4b010f3f1d21d30

Freshman 15: College Weight Gain Is Real. (2009, July 28). WebMD. https://www.webmd.com/diet/news/20090728/freshman-15-college-weight-gain-is-real#:%7E:text=A%20new%20study%20shows%20that,pounds%2C%20during%20their%20first%20semester.

Harvard Health. (2021, April 12). *Playing with the fire of inflammation.* https://www.health.harvard.edu/staying-healthy/playing-with-the-fire-of-inflammation

Hess, A. J. (2021, September 9). *The U.S. has a record-breaking $1.73 trillion in student debt—borrowers from these states owe the most on average.* CNBC.

https://www.cnbc.com/2021/09/09/america-has-1point73-trillion-in-student-debtborrowers-from-these-states-owe-the-most.html

How to keep a mental health journal. (2022, May 11). MHA Screening. https://screening.mhanational.org/content/how-keep-mental-health-journal/?layout=actions_ah_articles,light

The importance of hydration. (2018, June 22). News. https://www.hsph.harvard.edu/news/hsph-in-the-news/the-importance-of-hydration/

Keep an Eye on Your Vision Health. (2020, October 1). Centers for Disease Control and Prevention. https://www.cdc.gov/visionhealth/resources/features/keep-eye-on-vision-health.html#:%7E:text=Improving%20your%20eyesight%20is%20important,early%20and%20preserving%20your%20vision.

Keep Your Brain Young with Music. (2022, April 13). Johns Hopkins Medicine. https://www.hopkinsmedicine.org/health/wellness-and-prevention/keep-your-brain-young-with-music

Mejia, Z. (2018, May 3). *Just 10 minutes of exercise a week can make you significantly happier.* CNBC. https://www.cnbc.com/2018/05/03/just-10-minutes-of-exercise-a-week-can-significantly-make-you-happier.html#:%7E:text=Generally%2C%20the%20type%20of%20exercise,in%20less%20time%2C%20researchers%20found.

Mental Health Organization. (2016, June 7). *Mental health statistics: children and young people.* Mental Health Foundation. https://www.mentalhealth.org.uk/statistics/mental-health-statistics-children-and-young-people

Nair, M. (2022, February 23). *How to Avoid Student Loan Debt? Useful Tips!* University of the People. https://www.uopeople.edu/blog/how-to-avoid-student-loan-debt/

Powell, F., Kerr, E., & Wood, S. (2021, September 17). *What You Need to Know About College Tuition Costs.* US News. https://www.usnews.com/education/best-colleges/paying-for-college/articles/what-you-need-to-know-about-college-tuition-costs

Reading information aloud to yourself improves memory of materials. (2017, December 1). ScienceDaily. Retrieved June 27, 2022, from https://www.sciencedaily.com/releases/2017/12/171201090940.htm

Student Loan Hero. (2022, April 6). *A Look at the Shocking Student Loan Debt Statistics for 2022.* https://studentloanhero.com/student-loan-debt-statistics/

Sun, L. U. T. (2018, October 13). *Online food delivery market could grow to $24B by 2023: A Foolish Take.* The Motley Fool. https://eu.usatoday.com/story/money/food/2018/10/13/online-food-delivery-grubhub-ubereats/38089847/

Tefft, B. (2016, December). *Acute Sleep Deprivation and Risk of Motor Vehicle Crash Involvement.* Foundation for Traffic Safety. http://publicaffairsresources.aaa.biz/wp-content/uploads/2016/11/Acute-Sleep-Deprivation-and-Risk-of-Motor-Vehicle-Crash-Involvement.pdf

University of the People. (2022). *How to Avoid Student Loan Debt? Useful Tips!* https://www.uopeople.edu/blog/how-to-avoid-student-loan-debt/

Upham, B. (2019, September 25). *Large Study: Low-Intensity Activity Has Health Benefits.* EverydayHealth.Com. https://www.everydayhealth.com/fitness/large-study-light-intensity-activity-health-benefits/

van Hise, K. (2017, March 13). *Put Your Digital Devices to Bed Early: Optometrists Caution Overexposure to Blue Light May Cause Health Issues|EyeCare.org.* Eye Care Organization. https://eyecare.org/site/put-your-digital-devices-to-bed-early-optometrists-caution-overexposure-to-blue-light-may-cause-health-issues/#:%7E:text=The%20American%20Optometric%20Association's%20(AOA,day%20looking%20at%20their%20screens.

Wallis, A. (2020, June 24). *How Much Sleep Should a College Student Get?* Southern New Hampshire University. https://www.snhu.edu/about-us/newsroom/education/how-much-sleep-do-college-students-need#:%7E:text=well%20in%20school.-,According%20to%20the%20Centers%20for%20Disease%20Control%20and%20Prevention%20(CDC,in%20a%2024%2Dhour%20period.

Water Science School. (2019, October 22). *The Water in You: Water and the Human Body | U.S. Geological Survey.* USGS: Science for a Changing World. https://www.usgs.gov/special-topics/water-science-school/science/water-you-water-and-human-body#:%7E:text=In%20adult%20men%2C%20about%2060,their%20bodies%20made%20of%20water.

Yetman, D. (2020, October 8). *Is It Better to Sleep for 1 to 2 Hours, or to Not Sleep at All?* Healthline. https://www.healthline.com/health/is-2-hours-of-sleep-better-than-no-sleep#summary

Zhang, Z. (2018, March 24). *A Systematic Review of the Relationship Between Physical Activity and Happiness.* SpringerLink. https://link.springer.com/article/10.1007/s10902-018-9976-0?error=cookies_not_supported&code=c1fa2959-e7b0-4d7a-b01d-bbffe09d03cb

Introduction

Becoming an adult is incredibly exciting. We have freedom to choose how and where we will live our lives. It could be a time of exploring college options for some, while first jobs may be on the horizon for others. Whatever your case, if you are in your late teens and 20s, this is when you develop yourself, build your strengths, and work on your weaknesses. Because with greater freedom, comes greater responsibilities - not to mention a TON of new skills you'll need to master as a grown-up!

As an adult you have so many more choices. You can decide what and when to eat, where to live, and what time to go to bed. School taught you a lot, but there were many others that you will have to learn on your own. Maybe you can tell me what the capital of Estonia is, the stages of the water cycle, and the square root of 144. But none of those things will be helpful when you blow a tire, have trouble with your first landlord, or show an allergic reaction when living alone.

This is because adulting is not easy. It can be super challenging. And what we learn in high school, even though it is important, rarely gives us the answers to our everyday struggles when we start to be an "adult". We must deal with taxes, deadlines, laundry, eating healthy, exercising, getting enough sleep, etc. So it is ok to feel lost and overwhelmed at times. But the good news is that you're in the right place. We're going to cover all your adulting questions like…. How do I apply for a job? What should I wear to an interview? How do I choose where to live? When do I know fruit has gone bad? Where have all my socks gone?!

In the next pages, all your questions will be answered. You'll learn not only how to survive in a grown up world, but how to be a super successful adult too. So let's get started!

Part 1: Life skills & living away from home

One of the biggest changes you'll encounter is moving away from home. Most of us will move away at some point, for college or work. But how do you find the right home for you? What should you consider? Let's begin with a few important things to consider.

1. Renting

To successfully rent your first home, you must take several steps.

Choosing your location

The initial step when deciding where to get your first apartment/house is to choose zones of the city you like and discard those that you know won't fit your needs. Here are some things you should consider:

- Is it near shops or supermarkets? Can you walk to these or do you need a car?

- What about public transportation and parking spaces? Is there a place to park outside? Is it designated or how exactly does it work? Is your new home near a train station or bus stop?

- Are there bars around the area? If you're a party animal this might be perfect. But if you work shifts, you might not appreciate loud party noises late at night.

- Are you near parks, gyms, and other leisure places you consider important?

- Is it safe? Remember to check this at night also. You can best get to know a neighborhood by walking around it.

- How long will it take for you to travel each day to your work or college? If you hate commuting, you might need to find somewhere within walking distance. Or are you willing to live further away for a lower rent, but have a longer commute?

More than one area of your city is likely to fit your criteria for where you want to live, so the next consideration is the distance from your work/college.

Defining your budget

Knowing your budget is essential before choosing an apartment. The cost of renting will not only include rent, but also internet, food, transportation, heat, and other expenses.

In terms of a renting budget, the 30% rule is often used. According to this rule, we should spend no more than 25%/30% of our income on rent and expenses. Rent, services (gas, electricity, water, internet), and taxes will be included. Using this rule, you'll ensure you have enough money for your everyday expenses, such as food and transportation.

After determining how much rent you can afford, decide whether you will live alone or with a roommate and what type of apartment you will live in. In many cities, renting an entire apartment is incredibly expensive, so renting a room in a shared apartment may be the only option for many people.

Sharing vs. living alone

After reviewing your budget and clarifying how much you can spend on rent, you can choose what kind of home you would like to live in.

Determining how many bedrooms and bathrooms the apartment should have will depend mostly on whether you'll live alone or with someone else.

If the apartment is just for yourself, there are two things to have in mind: storage and working space. First, does the apartment have enough storage space for your things? And on the other hand, will you be working from home? If that's the case, it would be good if you considered an extra space so you can have a comfortable working area.

There is also the possibility that you decide to share the apartment with someone else. If that is the case, remember to prioritize big common spaces and a comfortable room for yourself. Whenever you share a house, your room becomes your space, so try to make it something you'd enjoy spending time in.

Sharing can be a great experience or a terrible one depending on how it is organized. It would be frustrating to wake up late for work and find there are two people in line ahead of you to take a shower. Crazy as that may sound, it happens more often than you think. The ideal situation would be for two people to share a toilet and three to share a shower.

But sharing an apartment can also be the best decision ever, and a way to make lifelong friends.

Viewing the apartment

When you're viewing the house or apartment, there are a few things to keep in mind.

- First, get an overall impression of the house. Is it clean and light? Is there any mold on the walls? Is the kitchen a mess? Does it look like the people who live there care about it? Walking into a dirty dark apartment is not a great start.

- If you will be sharing, find out who lives there now. Are they all college students who love to party? Are they professionals who work a lot? Are the people who stay there during the week but are not there much at the weekend?

- What is the situation with having friends or girlfriends/boyfriends over?

- What is the landlord like? Does he come around often? Is he good at getting things fixed when they break?

- What type of contract is required?

- Is a deposit needed and if yes, how much?

Signing the contract

Rental contracts usually require you to give the landlord a warranty concerning your ability to pay the rent in the future. Depending on the circumstances, you may be required to provide your income statements or a guarantor. You can always call a real estate office to find out the usual expectations regarding rental contracts in your city.

Finding the right home for you is not impossible, and the effort will pay off. With these simple steps, you will get a house that not only meets your needs but also does not stretch you financially. Once you're in it, it's a whole new chapter.

2. Moving in

After you have successfully rented your apartment (or room in a house share) and are satisfied with the results, the time has come to fill it up. If you are in a room share situation, you might only need to buy some of these - mainly things for your own room. If you are renting a house by yourself, you might need to invest in more items.

As general advice, buy consciously. If you don't want to find yourself in a year covered with stuff you don't use, buying consciously is essential. These are some points to keep in mind when shopping.

Buying furniture

Start with buying only the essentials. A piece of furniture to sleep on, another to sit on, to dine, etc. Here are some items to consider:

The bed

People's health depends on the quality of their sleep, as you know. We spend roughly a third of our lives sleeping. Would you want to spend that much time sleeping in an uncomfortable bed? The mattress market offers an enormous variety of options. Special foam is used in modern models that are incredibly durable and do not easily lose shape.

For the bed's structure, a simple one is always the best. Investing in a classic bed frame of neutral colors that will last a lifetime is a great idea. And by changing the duvet or pillows in your room, you can transform the look of it. In addition, it is also important to think about how much storage space you need. Also think how you will get this bed to your bedroom. Can it be moved in a few pieces? Will it fit up the stairs to your apartment? Don't forget to consider the logistics when you've found your super comfy bed!

Once you know the size of your bed, then you'll also need sheets, pillows, pillow covers and either a duvet or blankets that match your bed size. Two of each is a good idea as you can use one set while the other set is in the wash.

Sofa

Since we spend most of our time in the living room, the sofa is like the heart of the house. Our sofas are more relevant than we think, whether watching movies or TV shows, getting together with friends, or relaxing after work.

As with the bed, the recommendation is to choose neutral colors and a classic design so you don't have any problems changing the apartment's decor in the future. A sofa with a washable cover is a great idea too.

Storage

The fastest way to declutter your home or bedroom, is to buy some storage units and tidy things up. Buying one or two useful storage units for your home is one of the most practical and useful things you can do!

The best place to buy furniture

When buying your first pieces of furniture, Flat pack furniture is what I recommend you go for.

The first thing that stands out about this type of furniture is that it is the most affordable you can get on the market. This is because their large-scale production makes them cheaper and easier to manufacture. Additionally, they're cheaper because they compensate for their lower durability, but if you take care of them, they'll last a long time.

Shipping, assembly, and disassembly are easy. Because customers pick their furniture and build it in their homes, companies don't have to pay huge shipping costs.

It is possible to customize flat packs, there are numerous websites and hacks that can be used to improve or change the design. By doing so, people can make a cheap flat-pack look more expensive and luxurious for very little money.

Packing and moving this type of furniture is easy. You can easily transport your furniture and reassemble it when you move house by disassembling it, packing it in its flat boxes, and putting it in the moving truck.

- Extra: Kitchen implements

In the kitchen, you'll need the utensils for day-to-day use, things like plates, cutlery, and glasses. Even though these are important, the good news is you don't have to spend too much on them. The first days after moving would be tough without these things, so they should be a priority.

Now that we have your bedroom sorted and kitchen items ready, the supermarket is the next place you should visit.

Your first grocery shop

When you get home the first time, you'll need to visit the grocery store immediately since the fridge and pantry are empty. Here's some advice for making your first grocery shop a success.

Set a budget for the purchase

The key to saving personal finances is to know how much money you can or should spend on the shopping basket. It will be much easier for you to control spending and waste if you create a budget for food, whether it is monthly, weekly, or daily.

Prepare your shopping list before you go grocery shopping.

Adding more than you need to your shopping basket can make your grocery bill skyrocket. If you haven't planned your purchase, it is easier for this to happen. Before shopping, check your pantry and think about the meals you will prepare for that week, so you will know what you need. Once you have a list of all these items, limit yourself to buying only the items on it. This way, you will avoid getting too carried away by cravings and spontaneously buying unnecessary things.

Buy at the cheapest supermarket

The store you make your purchase may impact your spending more than you realize. It is important to understand that when identifying the cheapest supermarkets, it is about finding the best prices (which saves you money), not the one with the most offers. Ask your friends or work colleagues to find some good value supermarkets in your area, or check what's close by on Google maps.

Try using an online supermarket price comparator

The advantage of shopping online is that you don't have to go to the supermarket. When you don't have to navigate endless aisles of items, you're more likely to stick with the products you need.

Furthermore, it is also easier to compare their prices and choose the one with a lower price. There are several online supermarket comparators to help you with this.

Buy seasonal goods

You can save on your purchase by purchasing seasonal products since they are cheaper.

When the climatic conditions are right for their cultivation, they can be produced easily and supplied in greater abundance, lowering their price.

Check best before dates

Food usually has a limited life span. So check the date on all food items before you purchase. There's no point buying lots of chicken if it will all be out of date tomorrow. But if you know you will be eating your food the same day, sometimes you can get good bargains on items that are coming up to their use by date.

Give White Labels a Chance

It's well-known that white brands are less expensive, so purchasing them at the supermarket will save you money. Even though private label products tend to cost less, some nutrition experts advise against them. The best way to ensure the quality of these items is to always check the ingredients.

Use coupons and loyalty cards to save money.

Getting a loyalty card can be a good idea since shopping is almost inevitable, and you tend to go to the same shops almost every day. Their members are provided with certain benefits, such as the classic coupons they can use to get items at a better price.

Avoid prepared products

You will generally pay more for precooked and prepared dishes than if you bought the ingredients separately.

Items such as tomato sauce, grated cheese, cut vegetables, etc., are similarly affected. This is a common selection of products in a shopping basket, but the truth is that they will raise your final bill more than if you buy fresh tomatoes, cheese, or vegetables and prepare them yourself.

Buy in bulk

Sometimes, we come across large packages containing many units of the same product and think they are too big and take up too much space. This is a shame because large formats are usually cheaper.

This can be solved by sharing it with someone, like your neighbor, family member, or friend. It's also a good idea to buy items in bulk that you can store and use over time, like toilet paper or cleaning products. This will only take up a little space.

Compare prices per kilo or per liter, not per unit

By taking advantage of the fact that usually, the largest format is typically the cheapest, some chains put higher prices on packages with more units, even when they can theoretically save money. To avoid this, it is important to check the cost per unit/liter/kilo, which is expressed in smaller letters on the same price tag.

Beware of items near the checkout

You will often find attractive products such as trinkets or magazines at the checkout stand and practical items such as light bulbs or batteries. Since these items are not very expensive, they are easy to add to a basket in a last-minute impulse purchase while waiting for payment. It will cost you a few more dollars to do this.

Have fun with your first shop! The most important thing is to remember that every mistake when living alone is an opportunity to learn and buy better in the future. In a few days, keep a note of what you forgot to buy, or what you didn't buy enough of, and update your weekly shopping list with this info. This will save you time and hassle in the future and streamline your shopping each week. You can also see if any stores do free online delivery, and save some extra time by ordering your food to be delivered each week.

Basic grocery list

A list is an essential tool we must have at hand when going to the supermarket because it will help us plan and control the expenses incurred to stock up on food, utensils, and cleaning products for home and personal use. Not having a shopping list often leads to impulse purchases and forgetting the important stuff.

The following is a compilation of basic products, there is no need to buy them all, but you can create a list of what you need and make it as detailed and accurate as possible.

Groceries

- EGGS
- PASTA (SPAGHETTI, LASAGNA, PENNE, ETC.)
- BAGGED SOUPS (STARS, LETTERS, ETC.)
- BOXED CEREAL
- WHEAT FLOUR
- CORNMEAL
- PANCAKE FLOUR
- GROUND BREAD
- MAYONNAISE
- MUSTARD

- BOXED MASHED POTATOES
- VEGETABLE OIL
- OLIVE OIL
- COOKING SPRAY
- VINEGAR
- CHOCOLATE POWDER
- CHOCOLATE BARS
- JELLIES
- BAKING SODA
- JAMS
- COOKIES
- HOT SAUCE
- WORCESTERSHIRE SAUCE
- SOY SAUCE
- TOMATO SAUCE
- DRESSINGS

Beverages

- WATER (PLAIN, FLAVORED, WITH GAS)
- SOFT DRINKS
- JUICES
- TEA (POWDER, SACHET, OR BREW)

Fruits and vegetables

- SPINACH
- LETTUCE
- CABBAGE
- PARSLEY
- CILANTRO
- BELL PEPPER
- BROCCOLI
- GARLIC
- ONION
- MUSHROOMS
- SERRANO PEPPER
- ANCHO PEPPER
- TOMATO
- TOMATO
- POTATO
- CARROT
- PUMPKIN OR ZUCCHINI
- CELERY
- TAMARIND
- SEASONAL FRUIT
- LEMON
- APPLE

- WATERMELON
- BANANAS
- AVOCADO
- PAPAYA
- ORANGE
- RED FRUITS
- CUCUMBER
- PLUMS
- BLUEBERRIES

Cooking essentials

- REFINED SALT
- GRAIN SALT
- PEPPER
- GARLIC POWDER
- OREGANO
- CINNAMON
- THYME
- ROSEMARY
- PAPRIKA
- TURMERIC
- ACHIOTE
- CUMIN

- SAFFRON
- CHICKEN BOUILLON CUBES
- BEEF BOUILLON CUBES
- BASIL
- VANILLA
- DRIED LAUREL
- CHILI POWDER

Canned food

- TUNA
- SARDINES
- BEANS TO TASTE
- POWDERED MILK
- CONDENSED MILK
- EVAPORATED MILK
- CHIPOTLES
- RAJAS
- VEGETABLES
- CORN FLAKES AND
- FRUITS IN SYRUP

Grains and cereals

- BEANS
- RICE
- LENTILS
- OATS
- FLAXSEED
- CORN

Meat, chicken, fish and seafood

- STEAK
- CHOPS AND GROUND BEEF (PORK OR BEEF)
- CUTS OF BEEF TO TASTE
- LAMB
- CHICKEN BREAST
- CHICKEN THIGH AND LEG
- FISH FILET
- SHRIMP
- SALMON
- PORK OR TURKEY HAM
- PORK OR TURKEY SAUSAGE
- BACON

Sausages and dairy

- MILK
- SOY MILK
- ALMOND MILK;
- CHEESE
- CREAM CHEESE
- SOUR CREAM
- BUTTER
- MARGARINE
- CHORIZO
- SALAMI

Personal maintenance

- TOILET SOAP
- SHAMPOO
- CONDITIONER
- HAIR GEL
- DEODORANT
- SANITARY NAPKINS
- TOILET PAPER
- TOOTHPASTE
- TOOTHBRUSH
- BODY AND FACE CREAM
- SHAVING FOAM

- RAZOR AND RAZOR BLADES
- DIAPERS
- DISPOSABLE TISSUES AND
- MAKEUP

General cleaning and others

- NAPKINS
- ABSORBENT TOWELS
- ALUMINUM FOIL
- PLASTIC WRAP
- GARBAGE BAGS
- FIBER AND SPONGE FOR DISHES
- DISHWASHING SOAP
- DEGREASER
- BROOM
- DUSTPAN
- BUCKET
- JARS
- RAGS
- LAUNDRY SOAP (LIQUID, POWDER, OR BAR)
- DRAIN CLEANER
- FLOOR CLEANER
- CHLORINE

- GLASS CLEANER
- LIGHT BULBS
- CANDLES
- MATCHES AND/OR LIGHTER
- BATTERIES
- GLOVES

Once you've got a complete grocery list, you can go shopping knowing that nothing is missing from your house when you get home. Remember, buy frozen and refrigerated foods last.

Cleaning basics

One of your roles as an adult is not - cleaning! And you're about to find out that there are about a million different household cleaning products. Dust cleaners, window cleaners, all-purpose cleaners, floor cleaners, disinfectors, and degreasers are available for all sorts of uses. But is it really necessary to spend so much on them, or is it just a matter of accumulating unnecessary cans?

Cleaning products

To keep each area of your house in perfect condition, including the dishes, stove, furniture, and others, you will need the necessary utensils. Many cleaning products are unnecessary, so let's go through the ones that are necessary and why.

The basics

Depending on your type of floor (tiles, carpet, lino or wood), you will have to get a product that helps you keep it in perfect condition. Brooms, dustpans, and mop buckets are a good place to start.

Gloves, rags, and fibers to consider

- A soft cloth (better microfiber) to clean the dust.

- A cloth for cleaning the kitchen, one for the countertop every day and another for the hob.

- In the bathroom, you need a pair, one for the toilet and another for the rest of the fixtures and surfaces.

- An extra one to clean window panes, for example, might be a good idea.

- When cleaning, don't forget to protect your hands. Gloves are always helpful.

Kitchen products to consider

- Dishwasher detergent or dishwasher machine detergent (specific to this appliance). Add polish and salt if you live in an area with hard water.

- Disinfectant (antibacterial) for cooking surfaces. Ammonia and water for tiles.

- Clean hoods and other areas with degreaser.

- Floor cleaner liquid

- Window cleaner

- Antibacterial surface cleaner

Laundry products to consider

- A good detergent and softener for your clothes.

- Specific products for removing sweat stains and odors.

Bathroom products

- A specific cloth for the toilet area.

- WC bleach and a cleaning agent that won't damage the enamel of the toilets or the taps (use a soft cloth, not a scouring pad).

- An anti-limescale cleaning spray can be used to remove stubborn stains on shower screens.

- Glass cleaners work better on mirrors.

- For the floor, a water-diluted floor cleaner.

Cleaning routine

The key to a happy life is a tidy home; dividing the cleaning into daily, weekly, and monthly tasks is easy to achieve. Organizing your tasks according to how often they should be done will help you avoid forgetting anything. Here is a sample cleaning schedule.

Daily cleaning

There are a few things you have to do every day. You should place clean utensils in cabinets and drawers in the kitchen, then dirty dishes should be cleaned or put in the dishwasher if you have one. Using this method, your sink will always be clear.

You will also need to clean leftover food with a scourer or a cloth so that they do not accumulate and end up smelling unpleasant later. After that, clean the countertop and glass ceramic and vacuum if necessary.

Make sure the living room is tidy, pick up newspapers, books, empty coffee cups or magazines that are strewn about.

Open the bedroom windows in the morning to ventilate and pick up any clothes or shoes on the floor. Finally, air out the sheets and bedspreads. Make sure to store them in the corresponding drawers and cabinets; when you do this daily, you will always have everything perfectly arranged.

Although the bathroom needs to be deep cleaned every week, you should superficially clean it every day. This involves passing over the sink, the toilet, the shower, and the screens more than anything else.

Taking out the garbage daily will also be necessary, especially if it is organic, to prevent it from smelling. The inorganics will also be disposed of every few days, along with the glass and cardboard, in their respective containers.

Weekly cleaning

Consider taking advantage of a couple of hours on weekends to thoroughly clean the house so that it remains in perfect condition throughout the week. Unlike daily cleaning, weekly cleaning requires thoroughness and dedication.

With daily cleaning, the kitchen will stay clean, but you have to vacuum and mop all corners of the floor every week. Additionally, it will be time to focus on appliances used daily and are easy to clean, such as the oven or microwave. By passing a cloth with a special product inside both appliances, you can prevent them from getting too dirty and prolong their useful life. It will also be necessary to give the exterior of the extractor kitchen a pass during the weekly cleaning, reserving the interior for the monthly cleaning.

In the living room, it's time to shake out the blankets and pillows as well as vacuum and dust the table, bookcase and shelves. You can also take this opportunity to clean out newspapers, magazines, and old papers that you no longer need and that get in the way. Fresh flowers will brighten your week when you put them in a vase.

It is also important to thoroughly clean the bathroom, paying particular attention to the shower tiles, the mirror, and the floor. Following the daily cleaning plan, you won't have to spend too much time cleaning the sink, shower, and toilet.

You might consider putting your dirty clothes in the washing machine over the weekend. Washing the towels and changing the sheets every week is also recommended. Additionally, if you iron clean clothes once a week, you will prevent them from accumulating.

Dust all surfaces and shelves in the house with the vacuum while not forgetting the door frames and paintings that hang on the walls.

Monthly cleaning

According to many experts, certain appliances should be thoroughly cleaned at least once a month. By doing so, they can be kept in good working order for a longer period of time.

Extractor hoods must be disassembled and cleaned inside and out with hot water and steam, as well as the filters with anti-grease products. To prevent limescale and dirt accumulation, it is also important to wash the washing machine and the dishwasher periodically. Many models offer a special program for washing the appliance.

You may also want to review the fridge in great detail. Remove all expired food from the fridge and throw it away. After this, clean the interior and trays of the freezer to remove any leftovers, and make sure you go over the freezer.

Both inside and outside of window panes need to be cleaned regularly. The market offers a wide range of products suitable for this purpose and special tools that are enhanced to make your work easier.

Season cleaning

As the seasons change, it is time for a more specific cleaning, such as wardrobe changes: putting away the clothes you no longer need and bringing out the ones you'll start using.

If you have plants, you can also take the opportunity to prune them and remove dead leaves. If you have a garden, it is time to remove the leaves and branches, clean the weeds, and do not hesitate to give it a new look by planting fresh flowers.

If it is present, a parquet must be properly maintained to keep its beautiful appearance. Pass the mop over the floor using the products specifically designed for this type of flooring, then apply a layer of wax to make it look shinier.

Annual cleaning

Spend one or two days yearly on areas of the house that don't typically get cleaned very often but where dirt accumulates.

As for the kitchen, remove any packages or cans of food that have passed their expiration dates from the cupboards and discard them. After cleaning, use a cloth and soap to clean the surface thoroughly. Continue cleaning the cabinets and drawers where you store your plates, glasses, and cutlery. Make sure you do not overlook any corner.

Remove all the clothes from your closets, both in the rooms and the hallways, and put all the clothes and shoes you don't use in boxes to donate or throw them out if they are in poor shape. Additionally, while the wardrobe and its shelves are empty, make sure to clean them thoroughly. The best time to do this cleaning is during the summer or winter wardrobe change.

If your curtains or blinds are made of fabric, you can wash them in the washing machine and air out your carpets, mattresses, and pillows. If something does not fit in the washing machine, you can wash it in the bathtub or take it to a dry cleaner.

3. Laundry, house maintenance tips & more

Doing laundry

Knowing how to wash clothes in the washing machine is the first step to keeping clothes looking new for a longer period and also extending the life of your washing machine. The secret is to avoid a few mistakes that we make due to ignorance or routine, and we will save time, resources, and, in the end, money.

Avoid these five laundry mistakes:

1) Overfilling the washing machine with clothes. The drum should be filled a little more than three-quarters, with your hand fitting between the clothes and the drum walls. If you fill it too much, the clothes may not stir well enough and may not come out clean.

2) Ignoring the purpose of each compartment for detergent, fabric softener, and bleach. It is essential to pour each product in its place to avoid blending, which can ruin fabrics. You should also follow the level signals and not overdose.

3) Adding more detergent than necessary and not selecting the right washing cycle. Dose according to the manufacturer's instructions based on the dirtiness and hardness of the water. By adding more product, you are not washing better. On the contrary, traces of detergent or fabric softener may remain on the clothes, so you will need to rewash them. If your clothes are lightly soiled, wash them in short cycles and cold water; if they are very soiled, wash them in longer and higher temperatures.

4) Do not classify clothes before washing them. For the best cleaning, separate the garments by color (white, color, black) and similar fabrics.

5) Not reading labels (especially if it is a new garment). Labels inform us about temperatures; machine, dry or hand wash; bleach tolerance. Don't take anything for granted. If you are careless, you could ruin a garment. Here is a list of some common washing symbols you'll find on clothes:

- Machine wash

- Hand wash
- Do not wash
- Do not bleach
- Water temperature 30 degrees
- Iron
- Do not iron
- Tumble dry
- Drip dry
- Dry flat
- Dry clean
- Do not dry clean

How to boil an egg

This sounds simple but it's a very important life skill! If you can boil an egg you can make a very fast meal. So here is how to do it. Bring some water and a little salt to a boil in a pot. Make sure there is enough water to cover the egg.

Bring to the boil then reduce the heat to a gentle simmer for 3-5 minutes. Different people like different consistencies to their hard boiled egg. A 3 minute egg will still be a little runny. A 5 minutes egg will be less runny. Experiment with how you like your egg cooked.

You can also cool down your egg, and eat it later by soaking it in cold water for a little while, until it is cooler and then you can remove the shell.

How to know when food has gone off

Your senses can detect food spoilage as food becomes rancid or moldy when it spoils, and you can smell, taste, or see this before it becomes unsafe to eat. The general rule is that when food looks gone off, it is best to discard it. If in doubt, throw it out. Food poisoning is quite nasty and should be avoided. There are several things to look out for, including bad smells, slimy and greenish coatings, or mold on the surface. Very dark colors in the meat, soft skin in the fish, lumps in the flour, bruises or soft parts in the fruit and vegetables are signs that this food is in poor condition and should not be eaten.

How to iron a shirt

When ironing any part of the shirt, you should ensure that the fabric is well stretched. If you iron the wrinkle instead of removing it, you will worsen it.

Start at the inside of the shirt collar. Slide the iron over the wrinkled areas from one end to the other. Flip the shirt over and repeat the process. Lastly, fold in half and pass it through the iron several times.

Then, carefully stretch the shirt on the surface, and remove the wrinkles near the neck.

You can then iron the open cuffs by undoing the button so you don't have a line in the middle.

Next, you finish ironing the sleeves and accommodate the fabric by taking the sleeves by their internal seams and ensuring that both sides are flat before starting.

Then, iron the back, with the shirt open, and then the front.

Iron around the buttons rather than over them when ironing since you might burn and destroy them.

How to change the battery in a smoke alarm

The first thing you need to do is check the type of battery your detector uses. When you don't have the factory manual, you can google your device and see what battery it needs. Or after you remove the current battery and get another similar one.

Changing a battery requires you first to check if the detector is connected to an electricity network. If it is, you must disconnect the power from the network to work safely. Next, you must remove the smoke detector, usually by unrolling or sliding the cover, depending on the model. After you have opened it, you should identify where the battery is located and remove it. Pay attention to which way the battery is placed, as you must insert the new one the same way.

Make sure the battery you put in works before putting the cover back. Check to see if there is any light that indicates the equipment is on or if there is any sound that indicates it is already working. Put the cover back on the detector to finish. Never stay in a house without a working smoke detector, as it may save your life.

How to fix your toilet

A toilet can present several problems, so if you don't want to spend a lot of money calling a specialist, you should try fixing it yourself first.

One issue that can arise is the toilet getting blocked and not flushing anymore. This is usually because someone has put something they shouldn't down the toilet - like sanitary towels or wipes etc. Use a plunger a few times to loosen any materials that might be clogging the toilet.

If your toilet doesn't flush, also check the tank to see if it has enough water. Maybe it's a water issue. The handle on your toilet you push to get it to flush could also have broken. A common symptom is that water gushes out of the bowl, and in this case, you need to check whether the discharge mechanism or the water inlet mechanism has been damaged. In either case, the tank must be opened to check its contents.

You should fix the inlet mechanism if the water level is above the discharge level since it does not break when it should, and water continues to enter despite being full. On the other hand, if the water level is below the discharge level, the outlet mechanism must be faulty.

As plastic pieces are used daily, it is difficult to fix them once they break. It is important to identify which part of the equipment is broken in this case so that you do not have to replace everything. You can try adjusting its parts and position if you identify which part isn't working, but if you notice a broken part, the best solution is to replace the entire mechanism.

Part 2: Productivity, health and relationships

On a flight, when suddenly the cabin becomes depressurized, we are told to put on a mask first, then assist others, right? The same goes for your well-being in everyday life. Thinking about projects, relationships, jobs and long term goals is very difficult if you don't know how to take care of yourself on a day to day basis. A healthy mental and physical life, routines that fit your needs, and learning to create valuable relationships in which you can be yourself will provide a great foundation from which to grow and succeed.

1. Health

The difference between "healthy" and "sick" was evident as a child. If a doctor and some medicine were involved, you were sick. The rest of the time, you are healthy. As you grow older, you realize that health is a little more complicated. Anxiety, stress, allergies, where do we put them? It's hard to draw the line.

That's why it is important to remember that health isn't just the absence of disease, it's also a state of physical, mental, and social well-being. And to live a healthy life, we need to prevent, not react.

The power of self-care

Self-care comprises all those habits and attitudes we can perform to preserve and improve our health daily.

Self-care is equal to training your muscles to prevent injury during a race. Making simple changes in your daily habits will strengthen your system and health. Here are some of the changes you can consider.

Eat real food

Make a variety of fruits, vegetables, proteins, and whole grains the foundation of your diet. Batch cooking and an organized kitchen will help you achieve this.

Be consistent about when you eat. Skipping meals is not healthy long term, causing you to consume far more food than is necessary at the next meal, or snacking on unhealthy options. Considering our pace of life today, this can sometimes seem difficult, but it's something you need to prioritize.

Between meals, avoid snacking, or choose healthy snacks, such as non-fried nuts or fruit that provide essential nutrients.

Hydration is key. Besides helping to eliminate toxins, water aids digestion and prevents constipation. It is recommended to consume two liters of water each day.

Having a large bottle you can take with you everywhere and use as a measuring device to track how much water you drink is the easiest way to achieve this. Water, not soft drinks or sugary juices. In case you aren't used to drinking water regularly, adding a few slices of cucumber or lemon to your water bottle to flavor it can make it easier to drink.

Finally, nutrition must be cut back on very processed foods, which are high in trans or saturated fats, and consume foods with polyunsaturated fats, such as salmon, vegetable oil, nuts, or seeds. Don't forget, we truly are what we eat, so will you base your diet on junk food?

Sleep well

Getting rest is vital for our body to function properly. As well as affecting our hormonal, immune, and respiratory systems, poor sleep can also affect our blood pressure and cardiovascular health.

In addition, several investigations show that not sleeping can increase the risk of obesity, infections, and coronary diseases.

Sleeping well is more than just getting between 7 and 9 hours of sleep (the recommended hours of rest). It involves having a regular time to go to bed and wake up, having a bedtime routine (like brushing your teeth, taking a bath, or reading), and not drinking coffee or caffeinated beverages after 4 pm. Also, sleeping in comfortable clothes in a dark, quiet room is key.

If you find it difficult to fall asleep early and usually stay up late, there are two changes you can make. When the sun comes down, pause using screens and social media. They usually hyper-activate us, so if you use your phone less, you'll see how the need for resting appears. Also, try to have dinner two hours earlier than bedtime, and dim the lights after you do so. If you do this consistently, they will turn into signals for your body to know that resting time is coming soon and help it relax.

Move your body

A healthy lifestyle relies heavily on sport. If you think you do not have time or are not ready to start intense physical activity, you can start with baby steps, such as walking for short periods or stretching in the morning. Keep your muscles active by walking around. Make sure you get up every 60 minutes if you spend lots of time sitting.

Moderate long-term physical activity daily will bring many benefits, such as helping you control your blood sugar level, reducing the risk of coronary heart disease, promoting sleep quality, and increasing mindfulness in your body.

Over time you can increase the intensity of your sport. Learn to listen to your body. Don't force or strain your body. Wear equipment that is appropriate for the sport you practice. Good shoes and breathable clothing are essential.

Alcohol: Be careful

The annual death toll from alcohol worldwide is 3 million. The WHO reports the harmful effects of the abuse of alcohol, which is associated with over 200 pathologies and can lead to mental and behavioral disorders.

When it comes to consuming alcohol, moderation is key. Nutritionists and healthcare providers recommend limiting alcohol to social events or weekends, not over two units per event. Also, it is essential to drink water interspersed with alcohol.

If you drink alcohol during the week, do not have over one unit daily. The unit of drink constitutes a medium-sized beer or wine glass.

Be mindful of your hygiene

One of the good things COVID-19 has left us is the consciousness of the role of personal hygiene in preventing diseases. Good personal hygiene and cleanliness are a must, especially at home.

Washing your hands must be a part of your routine. This includes after traveling, before you eat, and after spending time with animals.

If you practice physical exercise or move around the city, it is good to shower daily to control germs that may affect your skin.

Also, changing your sheets and towels once a week will help you sleep in a clean environment and prevent allergies, skin breakouts, asthma, and other potential reactions related to the lack of regular cleaning.

Finally, if you live in the city, it is recommendable to incorporate the Asian custom of taking off your shoes and leaving them at the door when you get home. The pragmatic benefits are obvious: removing shoes keeps floors and carpets clean. But also, it will work as a reminder of the intention of keeping your home as a clean space.

Live slowly, prioritize mental health

As part of achieving physical health, mental health must also be considered. If one is not good, it will hurt the other and vice versa.

One of the main risks for our mental health today is stress. It is not only constantly present in our minds but drags us into loops of avoidance behaviors to "feel better," such as addictions, poorer diets, or sedentary life.

When it comes to taking care of your mental health, you can start by taking a few minutes off-line before starting your day. Connecting with what you feel, physically and emotionally, is key. Learn to accept yourself, and ask for help if you need it. Meditation is an excellent way to improve mental health and foster and nurture relationships with family and friends. Have one or more vital purposes for motivating yourself since having a long-term objective improves your mental health.

Self-care is less complicated than it seems. It is mainly about being conscious, being aware of what we put in our bodies (food, water, alcohol, screen time), and how we use it in our daily lives. Start by observing your everyday life to see what recommendations you could introduce to improve your well-being. Remember, "prevention is better than cure."

Health 101: Annual medical check-ups

When you get to your 20's, going to the doctor is on you. This means that it is your responsibility to take care of your health. Annual check-ups are the best way to ensure that we're healthy, treat diseases quickly, and keep our quality of life high.

After the summer, a check-up will show you how well you're doing so you can confidently return to your regular life. A complete medical check-up would include the following:

Clinical specialist

- Cholesterol control (if there are risk factors, otherwise they are done every five years)
- Diabetes screening (if risk factors present)
- Recommended vaccines
- Blood test
- Family history disease screenings
- Athletes: Examine the circulatory system and an electrocardiogram to detect anomalies related to sudden death.

Dermatologist

- Skin exam to check for lesions or moles that look suspicious

Sexual health specialist

- Men: Testicular exam
- Women: Pap smear, HPV vaccine, a breast exam.
- Screening for sexually transmitted infections (per patient request)

Mental health professional:
- If there's a history of emotional disorders, it is recommended.

Dentist:
- In time, you can solve cavities and gum problems.

Though it seems like a lot, it is only done once a year. Keep track of your health yearly, and there won't be any surprises. Through self-care and a yearly medical check-up, you will take the best approach to your health: prevention. As you improve your everyday habits, you will be confident that everything is going well by scheduling a check-up yearly.

If you're wondering if you win anything, the answer is; everything. Your body will be at its best, so you'll be closer to reaching your goals. The question is, what objectives are you setting for yourself?

2. Goal setting

If you are lost at sea, a map can be very useful, but you also need to know the name of the place you want to go to. The same thing happens in life. First we need to set our goals. What do we want to achieve in our career this year? What do we want to achieve in our personal lives in the next 12 months? What are our health goals for this year? When we know what our goals are, it's much simpler to then figure out a plan to get there.

SMART goals

Many adults spend their lives rushing from one job to another, from project to project, without ever feeling fulfilled by what they do. Usually, this happens because they accept what others ask them to do, rather than choosing their own direction for their life.

For example, I was a project manager in a tech company. I liked my job, but as the months passed, I became unhappy with the amount of overtime that was necessary.

During the summer, my boss called me into her office. She praised my work ethic, and said that if I continue on this path, there would be a promotion to senior project manager in my future, which would also include a raise in salary. Two months later, I had quit my job, as the small extra increase in salary, and a better job title would also have meant longer hours at the office and zero work life balance. But by knowing my life goals - to make a work life balance, and long term to move back to the country, saying no to a high profile job in the city was easy for me. And it was one of the best decisions I ever made.

SMART goals are an acronym that will guide your goal setting. Over time, you'll probably accomplish very little if you don't know where you want to go. Having clear ideas will turn into focused efforts and productive use of time and resources, increasing the chances of achieving what you want in life.

Specific: Your goals should be clear and focus on what you want. Simple and significant objectives are the ones we are looking for.

Measurable: We must measure how close we are to achieving our goals in order to make changes if necessary.

Attainable: The most common mistake when setting goals is aiming too high. Defining goals we can accomplish is basic for not feeling frustrated and giving up. Dividing the goals into smaller ones or in shorter periods is useful for achieving this. This doesn't mean we don't aim for the moon, we just start with baby steps on earth.

Realistic: Our goals should be something we can do. This does not equal an easy goal but an achievable one.

Time-oriented: The goals we set must be defined in time. This will clarify the processes and make it easier to understand the steps we must take to achieve what we want.

Using the SMART acronym when setting goals will help you gain clarity, focus, and motivation. Afterward, you should determine which goal matches your needs across the various areas of your life.

Divide and conquer: Goals by areas

There's a similar concept behind building an empire and creating who you want to be: divide and conquer. When setting goals, you need to identify what's important to you so you can create objectives that are consistent with what you value. A category distribution is a good system for goal setting. Here's some insight into different areas and some questions you can use to identify your goals.

Personal Development Goals

Personal and interpersonal skills are closely related to these types of objectives.

- What character traits would you like to develop?
- Are there any skills you want to master?
- What kind of friend do you want to be?
- What could you do for your physical well-being?
- Would you like to overcome your fear of public speaking?
- Would you like to be a better partner? Speak French? Or play the guitar?

As you can see, there are endless options for developing ourselves. Are languages, sports, and interpersonal skills you need to grow to be who you want to be?

Career/Financial Goals

Whether it's a career, business, or finances, these goals are related to what you want to have and be.

- Would you like to be a better leader and manage your teams better?
- What levels of financial abundance do you want to achieve?
- What position do you want to achieve in your company? Or do you want to become an entrepreneur and work for yourself?
- How much do you want to earn?
- Would you like to become the best salesperson in your company?
- If you are an entrepreneur or manager, what goals do you have for your organization?
- How far would you like to take it?

Adventure Objectives

There are two aspects to these goals - they are related to what you want to have and do on a playful level.

- What adventure and relaxed plan would you wish for most in the world?
- Travel to Australia?
- A house on the beach? A sailboat? A sports car?
- Stroll through New York?
- Go to a rock concert?

Contribution Objectives

These may be the most challenging and inspiring goals because this is your chance to make your mark on the world and "touch" other people's lives.

- Would you like to work at an NGO?
- Volunteering at a soup kitchen, helping to remove rubbish in your local area?

Once you have written down your SMART goals for each area of your life, it is time to return to the present. When setting them, we must remember that even though they are important, our goals are in the future, and the actual change occurs in the present. So, as we do with a compass, we look at them from time to time, so we don't get lost, but we get closer step by step.

In everyday life, those steps will bring us closer to our goals. Success is not an act but a habit.

3. Daily routines

Living alone - or even living with flatmates - can make time management somewhat problematic. We have all woken up five minutes before work starts. While it may happen occasionally, it's not a good way to impress your boss.

Living behind schedule always puts us in survival mode, far away from creativity and productivity. The best way to prevent this is to create a routine that fits your needs. Having a routine has solid benefits, like helping you grow personally, mentally, and pursue various goals.

If you don't have a routine yet, it is time to create one.

Discover your routine

When it comes to creating your routine, there are some things to take into consideration.

- Know what you want and why you want it.

- Be willing to experiment. Trial and error is the best way to find what works and develop it into what you need to continue to grow.

- Plan a small number of tasks instead of overloading your routine with too many things to do.

- Make sure your routine is aligned with your SMART goals, so you are sure your tasks correspond with what you're after.

- Don't make a big deal if you break the routine or habit. Accept yourself as a human, grow every day, and start over tomorrow.

What you need in your daily routine

Creating your routine can take a lot of time and energy, so it is essential to have specific points that will make your routine successful and fulfilling.

Daily Routine

- Early start
- Time to work out and exercise
- Meditation

- Eating times

- Work blocks

- Self-growth moments

- Hobbies and personal activities

- No screen time

1. An early start

How we manage our sleep time greatly impacts our health and quality of life. Many theories are floating around about which is better, being a night owl or an early bird. Part is this is figuring out which times we are most awake and productive. For example, my brain works best in the morning, it's when I can really focus and tackle my most difficult tasks. However, I don't naturally wake up early! So in order to reach my goals, I set an alarm and make sure the early morning sun comes into my bedroom, to help me wake up naturally too.

Different things determine your energy levels throughout the day, but usually most people are very energetic in the morning. By waking up early, you can take advantage of the most energetic hours of your day. This is also an ideal time for working out. You not only have the energy your muscles need to function at their best but your bodies are stimulated, allowing you to start the day with a clear mind.

Furthermore, starting your day early allows you to approach your day with some reflection (introspection) and planning. Setting aside a few minutes each morning to connect with yourself is important so you can create a realistic schedule based on how you feel and what you consider most important. Lastly, your sleep will benefit from following the natural circadian rhythm. Changing your habits might be hard, yet not impossible if you currently live more at night than early in the morning. It makes sense that you plan your activities in accordance with the cycle of light and darkness.

Light has an enormous impact on our circadian system. So if you wish to be a morning person, try reducing the light exposure at night and increasing it in the morning. This includes electronic devices such as tablets, computers, and cellphones.

Other cues, such as a consistent bedtime routine, can impact your circadian system. We do it with kids and babies, don't we? Baths, teeth brushing, and bedtime stories are all cues for them to understand that bedtime is getting closer. You can probably achieve a similar effect if you make yourself some tea or diffuse some oils before bed, even if you don't have somebody reading you a story or singing you a song.

As with other habits, you've got to be consistent in changing your sleeping patterns: "Start slowly, over a couple of days or weeks, and then keep at it until it sticks." It takes discipline but can be done.

2. A skincare routine

To get started with a skincare routine, there are many things you can do. As with anything, starting slowly is advisable if you've never applied products before. Here are the basics you can follow.

Cleansing

Ideally we should wash their faces every day! Sweat and sebum are produced during the day. It is not disgusting; it is necessary since an unprotected area of the face gets covered. But the skin is oily, so pollution, smoke, heavy metals, dust, and smog adhere to it.

Cleaning your face can be done in various ways, depending on your needs.

Cleaning oil: This is a staple of Korean skincare. A face oil (specially made for the face) is applied to the face and massaged gently to melt makeup and sunscreen. This oil does not adhere to the skin. Due to their formula, they emulsify upon contact with water, making them very easy to remove. You can find lots of different cleansing brands in your local drugstore or chemist.

Soap: You can use it every morning and night. It will remove makeup or sunscreen. If you find it harsh, consider a cleansing gel or balm.

In the evening, use micellar water or cleansing oil to remove your makeup, sunscreen, and dirt from the day. Ideally it's good to wash your face in the morning and evening.

Hydration/moisturizing

Hydration or moisturizing should be the second step in your skincare routine. How are they different? The first provides water to your skin, and the second provides oil to your skin. For a basic routine, let's begin with a moisturizer.

Which should I use? Just as with your other products, it depends on your skin type. Some moisturizing creams are designed for younger skin which may be more oily and prone to breakouts. Others are designed for dryer skin which has lost some of its elasticity. Always choose hypoallergenic products if you have sensitive skin.

Sun protection

All of us should wear sunscreen every day of our lives. No matter what the weather is like, where we are, even if it rains. Unlike other radiation, UV rays are powerful and can pass through walls, glass, and clouds. As a result, sunscreen is more than just a beach necessity.

And what are we protecting ourselves from? It's mainly from radiation that, in the long run, can cause skin cancer. Furthermore, we can prevent spots, wrinkles, and skin texture.

Perhaps you are under the impression that sunscreens are uncomfortable, greasy, heavy, and have white effects on the skin. Thanks to the hundreds of products on the market today, there is something for everyone, including sunscreens with a light texture, mattifiers, and some with colors. There is no reason for you not to protect your skin from the sun.

A correct skincare routine can be summarized in those steps. This may be a good place to begin if you have never used products on your face. Cleanse, hydrate, and use sunscreen in that order. You can apply makeup afterward. If not, you are well prepared to face the adversities of climate change and pollution, with your skin protected.

You can add other products like specific serums or oils as your routine evolves.

3. Time to work out

Experts recommend a minimum of 60 minutes of exercise every day. Considering how much time we spend sitting in front of computers each day, an hour is often not enough to compensate for our sedentary lifestyle's effects.

Exercise benefits all of your body's systems. Dopamine and other neurotransmitters will be released, giving you a sense of well-being throughout the day. Your mental health will improve, you'll have more clarity, and sleep better.

You can activate your digestive system by engaging in physical activity.

By satisfying that need with healthier food, you'll be able to get the most out of your workouts and trigger a cycle of well-being. You can also prevent gaining weight, heart disease, type 2 diabetes, and high blood pressure with regular exercise. Running or lifting weights can help strengthen your bones. Tennis is also a great way to stay fit and meet new people.

Also, it is good to include short workout blocks in your mornings. Training your strength, flexibility, or aerobics skills can take only 20 minutes of your morning, giving your body all the benefits previously detailed.

The most important thing about working out is to enjoy it. Those who find an activity they enjoy will stay consistent with it. In addition to the morning workout, you should try to incorporate it into your daily routine and make it a priority to find an activity you enjoy.

4. Meditation

John Lennon said it best: "Life is what happens to you while you're busy making other plans." Take a second to process this quote. Re-read it if necessary. What comes up inside of you? Is your mind where your feet are, or is it somewhere else?

It's just a moment that makes the difference: the moment we are there, registering what is happening in our lives, whatever it is. If we get distracted, the experience slips away. We could modernize John Lennon's quote: "Life's what happens to you while you're taking out your phone to take a picture."

The first lesson about mindfulness is that it's not about new experiences but new perspectives. True well-being comes from connecting directly with the source of that feeling, inside or outside ourselves. A mindful life is a happy life. And meditation can be a good way to exercise our mindfulness skills daily.

When we cannot find an answer to our problems, meditation offers another way. While meditating isn't a cure-all that will make the pain go away, it provides other benefits. For some, it can produce a sense of peace and determination. You can deepen your understanding through a flash of insight while meditating.

Here are some tips for incorporating it into your daily routine:

1. *What should you wear?*

Start by removing your shoes and getting into some loose garments. Let go of whatever tight clothing or loud accessories you are wearing and get into the meditation mood free of anything that can make the experience uncomfortable.

2. *Where should you do it?*

Meditation should be done somewhere you can feel comfortable and focus on the practice without getting distracted by stimuli from your surroundings. Your house, the park, your garden, the beach, anywhere can be a good spot if you feel it will allow you to slow down and connect with the present.

3. *How should you sit?*

Keep in mind that even if you dedicate a few minutes to it, if you maintain a bad posture to meditate, you will immediately feel discomfort from having your back loaded, your legs numb, or your arms flexed inappropriately, and this will distract you. Whether sitting on the floor or on a chair, keep your back straight but without tension, breathe deeply, and keep your shoulders and arms relaxed.

4. *What happens if thoughts interrupt you?*

When you meditate, different thoughts might arise, personal problems, discomfort at the time, or doubt about whether you are doing it right (which usually occurs when you first start). Accepting these thoughts is important.

Through meditation, we explore the idea that psychological well-being begins with accepting thoughts, emotions, and bodily sensations that simply cannot be changed or eliminated. If you have thoughts like this, accept them and return your attention to the object, breath, sound, or sensation.

5. *For how long should you meditate?*

As you begin to meditate, you should increase the time little by little. To improve your health and well-being, starting with a one-minute meditation is ideal and gradually progressing to 20 or 30 minutes of meditation daily.

Remember that meditation and relaxation should be a pleasant part of your day. Doing it with someone you love or in a place you enjoy will make it a worthwhile moment for you.

5. Time for food

The time we allot to food should be divided into two parts; time for cooking and time for eating. As for the first, cooking, the best alternative is to plan weekly and cook in batches. If you want to eat breakfast at the beginning of your day, schedule a time. Having breakfast before starting your day's work is the best way to get your day off to a good start.

At lunch and dinner, eat mindfully, plan your activities so that they don't interfere with these times, and try not to eat while you work or watch television. Being mindful of our diet allows us to make appropriate food choices. Our metabolism is an important reason we should eat at certain times each day. Nutrition and food experts believe humans must have a body clock that dictates what times to eat to avoid metabolic disorders and nutritional imbalances.

6. Work blocks

How often have you found yourself juggling many deadlines simultaneously in your job? Despite the pressure of being overworked and overburdened, there is a way to remain efficient. This is called time blocking.

Organizing time this way entails categorizing it into differentiating thematic blocks. This way, you know exactly what you must do during each work hour. Additionally, these thematic blocks allow you to structure tasks around a common thread without jumping from one activity to another. This saves us time and keeps us focused. Knowing a specific time is dedicated to a task, and nothing else, allows your mind to focus on what you are doing, which will free up your ability to think and create.

Organizing your work this way allows you to have a daily action plan, which will prevent you from missing deadlines for tasks that become urgent.

The most important aspect of structuring your work time in blocks is determining how much time is required for an action to be effective. In other words, determine how long each task will take. Otherwise, if you schedule your time unrealistically, you may experience the stress and frustration of having set yourself an impossible pace.

7. **Self-growth moments**

Similar to sports and meditation, self-growth will not happen without some time devoted to it in our schedule. To incorporate it into your daily routine, you must understand that it consists of two distinct components: unlearning and incorporating new ideas.

Unlearning means putting aside part of those models that inhabit our environments and that we have internalized to create something new. To do so, we need self-awareness and critical thinking skills, which we train when meditating.

And that's when incorporating new ideas comes into the picture.

By reading or listening to podcasts daily, your knowledge level will continue to grow and grow as you become more aware of new topics. You will learn new vocabulary, improve your spelling, and you will also be able to learn new things with each book, such as culture and history. The more we read, the more we discover.

Just by reading 20 minutes a day, you will see the difference. It does not have to be 20 minutes straight, it can be 10 minutes during the day and 10 minutes at night. This is approximately 20 pages per day, and although it may not seem like much, if you read 20 pages every day, you will have gotten to 140 pages in a month, you will have read more than 500 pages, and in a year 7000 pages. The average of books is approximately 300 pages; if you don't want to, you can read 25 books in a year. All you have to do is remain constant and dedicated to your personal development.

8. Hobbies and personal activities

Devoting time to yourself as a part of your daily routine might be the last thing you think of. However, you do need time to yourself in order to be able to thrive.

First of all, remember that you need to dedicate a few hours a day to pamper yourself. That can include reading, kickboxing, or any other hobby you choose. Thus, one of the main rules when it comes to hobbies is to realize that they are activities you enjoy and can use to feel motivated or happy throughout your day.

If you allow your free time to be used only to be productive, you'll feel unmotivated and stressed. As a society, we have adopted the idea that we need to be constantly productive or else we are wasting time. It's impossible to be productive every minute of the day, so resting or just doing stuff to relax shouldn't be something we feel guilty about.

9. Evenings off screen

As we're already aware, our body has its internal clock, which is controlled by hormones. When it gets darker, melatonin, a hormone that is naturally produced at night, begins to take over as the day's cortisol production slows down. Hormones like these let your body know it's time for bed.

Screens, such as smartphones, laptops, and TVs, emit blue light, which blocks the "sleepy" signals sent to your brain by melatonin. No wonder you don't have a good night's sleep when exposed to blue light at night.

Turning off screens before bed might be hard, but giving your mind and body a rest period without technology distractions is the goal. To achieve this, try to create a bedtime routine free of screens from start to finish, at least 30 minutes in length. As part of a healthy bedtime routine, the National Sleep Foundation recommends putting electronics away one hour before bedtime.

Devoting some time before you go to bed to prepare for the next day is an excellent way to stay conscious of your routine and daily activities. Set the clothes, put the kitchen in order, and take a moment to go through your schedule.

Finally, it's a good idea to take some time to reflect on your day before you go to sleep. Especially if you can capture your thoughts in writing. This way, you can refer the notes back to track changes over time and tweak your routine based on the real needs you observe.

Always leave room for growth and change

When constructing your routine, you must always ensure there is room for improvement and adaptation. Having a routine has great benefits, and you should take advantage of it. You may observe changes in your personal life, physical and mental health, and the pursuit of your goals.

But be open to the reality that things may need to be adjusted. The next time you notice something isn't working, hit the pause button, and ask yourself why. Don't be afraid of pausing, reassessing, and trying again. To achieve your goals, you must spend time thinking and incorporating them into your daily activities. This way you can reach your goals, be happy and create a life you love.

4. Relationships

Growing up brings many changes to our relationships. We meet new people as we enter new environments, such as the workplace. Friendships that were very close in our adolescence might lose strength. To feel fulfilled and build the relationships we want as we mature, we need some ideas about how to move in each area.

Love

As a general rule, adult relationships tend to be more satisfying than those during youth. As we mature, we enjoy greater emotional balance and well-being. As a matter of fact, experts say that the security and serenity that adult love provides can improve psychological and emotional health.

Mature love is beneficial because it has been worked on individually and as a couple. The intensity of our emotions separates a bond of this type from an adolescent one. Adolescents give themselves over and over again and lose perspective. As adults, we can respect each other's space and work together as a team.

The definition of an intimate relationship is two equal mature people who love each other, work together, share what they have in common, and respect what makes them different. It's a relationship built on interdependence, where they rely on each other equally, without it being a constraint. Each partner respects the other's individuality and accepts the other's behavior. Our differences in interests, values, or concerns will not be attributed to the absence of love or distance but rather to our individual differences.

When thinking about building personal relationships, we need to take into account the following principles:

- *Demarcation:* when two people form a voluntary relationship, they assume the relationship has priority over everybody else (friends, family, work). The couple is voluntary. The decision is made with the aim of having a positive and satisfying relationship between both parties.

- *Priority but not exclusivity:* the couple's relationship will not prevent us from being able to relate to and attend to other people who are important to us

- *Role flexibility:* As a couple, we will face different situations requiring us to adopt complementary roles. We will adjust to one another depending on the situation.

- *Equal value:* the two members of the couple are worth the same. For the simple fact of being alive, each person has intrinsic value.

- *Negotiation:* The ability to resolve conflicts to your satisfaction is a fundamental characteristic of a good relationship. This way, negotiations won't become a power struggle, where we may feel we are losing, but rather we'll be in it for the long haul. We're cooperating, and we're committed. So our willingness to "change" is more positive. To improve our flexibility, we will make changes with which we are comfortable, first and foremost for us. It'll be mutually beneficial in the long run. If a couple has problems, it will have an impact on them both. That's why it's important to look at it from both sides.

By keeping these principles in mind, you will be able to build a strong and valuable relationship and avoid toxic ones.

Work

Most of our adult lives are spent at work, in the organization we dedicate ourselves to. We all know that the quality of our work environment and relationships determine our willingness and motivation to tackle the tasks at hand. Our workplace relationships can also lead to friendships.

The whole organization contributes to the work environment. To improve the environment day after day, human resources managers must do their part, as well as collaborators, middle managers, and the basic workers. In light of this, the following five tips will help you maintain a healthy and valuable work relationship, enabling us to feel satisfied and happy.

- *Fluid communication:*

Good communication helps organizations reach their goals and boost productivity. It's essential for relationships. We should avoid talking about our colleagues and making negative comments behind their backs because that can damage communication and create problems.

When communicating with others, we must always be direct. It's also a good idea to avoid work issues in our free time, since learning how to improve the other aspects of our work relationships is important.

- *Do not blame other people:*

We're often not responsible for mistakes or problems the company as a whole commits because blaming third parties isn't our job. We can deal with this issue without having to accuse other people. Still, we should keep in mind that we're all human, and we all make mistakes, so let's not speak ill of anyone. We can start by assuming our role in the matter and helping the people who need it.

- *Share success:*

We should not feel bad or jealous of our colleagues and friends who succeed in achieving goals or completing a project before us. In fact, quite the opposite is true. We must be happy for others and learn from them to be able to apply their strategies on our own.

If other people's work is sincerely and positively valued, the climate and labor relations will be strengthened. In addition, this will demonstrate the team's great camaraderie and interest in achieving common success and avoiding rivalries or misunderstandings.

- *Positive attitude:*

As repetitive as it sounds, the attitude with which work is handled daily determines the success of all employee relationships. You should not transport personal problems to the workplace.

Your interest in others and friendliness will bring people closer together and improve the environment. The best way to make the day-to-day work in the organization excellent is by being cheerful and generating good conversations with everyone.

- *Help and allow:*

Sometimes you need others' opinions and help. It's then that we realize we have good relationships and how vital they are for a job well done.

We should make ourselves available to help others and let them help us when needed. Teamwork is best if you're looking to achieve goals, improve daily, and create a climate of respect and trust.

Friends

As social beings, we all need friends (there is even a national day to celebrate friends!). Nevertheless, the kinds of friendships we cultivate can change over time. Kids have a remarkable ability to call someone their friend. When they see a child their age at the park, they already consider him their friend, even though maybe they don't even know his name.

With age, this concept changes, and there are more conditions to consider someone a friend. When is someone considered a friend? A friendly relationship depends on two people finding something in common, an affinity, according to the RAE. It could be sharing a hobby, an activity, an experience, or simply having similar interests.

As human beings, however, we cannot remain static all the time. Just like our bodies, our experiences, interests, and priorities will also change in the future; as a result, our friendships will also change. Adapting is necessary in the face of these changes, which can sometimes result in a crisis. There is a pressing need for adjustment to this new situation, leading to two possible outcomes: that our bonds of friendship are maintained and remain through the storm; or that they break.

To maintain a relationship, both sides should have the real desire to do so. Healthy relationships require respect, tolerance, listening, and sincerity. Every friendship has its own level of demand and, therefore, requires its own level of care.

We all live in a world where relationships play a significant role in our everyday lives. As important as working on ourselves and our projects is, working on the bonds we have with the people we love is also important. To have a fulfilling life, we need more than "professional success," we need to share it with people we love.

5. FAQs and hacks

What to put in your first aid kit

The best thing to do in an emergency is to be ready. What should be included in a home first aid kit? Here is a list of some of the most important basic things you should include:

- Alcohol wipes or alcohol gel
- Antiseptics such as hydrogen peroxide and iodized solution.
- Band-aids or bandages of different sizes to cover the wound or control bleeding.
- Sterilized gauzes.
- Physiological serum.
- Sticking plaster.
- Scissors.
- Gloves.

In addition, your first aid kit should be kept in a clean, safe area. And of course, it should be accessible. Reviewing it at least twice a year to replace expired items is a must.

What to do in case of an allergic reaction

The first thing you should do is assess the severity of the allergy. This can be mild, such as an itchy mouth or skin or coughing from dust or pollen. Or it can be severe, such as large hives or patches on the skin or severe difficulty breathing. In the first case, it is ideal to identify what is causing the reaction and avoid contact with that substance. Not eating a certain food, avoiding using a particular cream, or simply closing the windows so that dust does not enter from the outside.

In the second scenario, the situation is complicated, so talk to someone more knowledgeable. The best option is to visit a doctor.

Which contraception method is best for you

To start with, you need to know that a condom is the only method that, in addition to preventing pregnancy, prevents sexually transmitted diseases, so it is very important that you use one.

Women can supplement protection with contraceptive pills that, in addition to preventing pregnancy, can also help you to reduce acne and hirsutism, regulate menstrual cycles, have less painful periods, and manage other conditions associated with menstruation.

Other methods, however, are more complex and require more dedication. Therefore, examining and analyzing them carefully is convenient before deciding on them. Among these are IUDs (Intrauterine Devices) that must be placed by a gynecologist, the diaphragm for women who do not want a hormonal method, or injectable contraceptives or contraceptive patches.

Why should you wear SPF daily?

The use of sunscreen is not limited to summer vacations or trips to the pool since exposure to the sun without protection has the same consequences all year long.

When walking to the supermarket or running in the park, you are less aware of it, which is when it harms you the most. In technical terms, the sun causes skin aging by forming free radicals, which destroy collagen fibers. As a result, wrinkles, sagging, dehydration, and spots can appear. Significantly higher exposures can result in skin cancer.

For all these reasons, starting to use sunscreen every day is a good choice.

How to treat a burn

Your treatment will depend on how severe the burn is. Burns are categorized according to their severity. The first degree is the least serious, affects the outer layer of the skin, and causes little pain, redness, and swelling. The second degree affects deeper layers and causes blisters. Third- and fourth-degree burns may damage joints and bones, which need to be treated in a hospital.

You should first put the affected area under cold water for about 20 minutes. As soon as the burning sensation has diminished, you should gently wash the burnt area with water and soap. At a later point, you can continue adding something cold every five to fifteen minutes, depending on the severity of the pain. For serious burns, you should seek medical attention asap.

CPR basics

When dealing with a person who can't breathe normally or if they are breathing heavily, knowing these steps can be beneficial since you can save their life. The first thing to do is contact an emergency service or request help while doing CPR.

To do the chest compressions, you must first find the center of the chest, placing two fingers at the junction of the ribs and the base of the other hand on top of the two fingers.

While pressing with the base of one hand and the other on top of it with the fingers intertwined, you should do about 100 compressions per minute, that is 1 or 2 per second, as long as the chest drops at least 2 inches (5 cm).

If this does not work, a more complex step must be performed, and you should have prior training for this. It takes 30 compressions followed by two breaths, and you must repeat this cycle as often as necessary until the patient can breathe by themselves.

SMART goals template

Specific: What exactly do I want to do?

_____
_____
_____
_____
_____

Measurable: How will I keep track of my progress?

_____
_____
_____
_____
_____

Attainable: Is this something I'm capable of?

_____
_____
_____
_____
_____

Relevant: What is the purpose of this? Is it important to me?

_____
_____
_____
_____
_____

Time-orientated: When will I complete this?

_____
_____
_____
_____
_____

How to identify friendships that empower you

When choosing friends, it is essential to know how to tell the difference between positive friendships and toxic ones.

Positive friend

- Encourages you to achieve your goals
- Cheers you on
- Shares in your happiness when you succeed
- Treasures your friendship.
- When you're together, you feel good about yourself
- A friend like this makes a positive difference in your life, and you also make a positive difference in his/hers.

Toxic friend

- Secretly sabotages your dreams and success by causing you to doubt.

- Is someone jealous of your relationship and wants to exploit it to manipulate you.

- You feel uncomfortable with him/her and conclude that it must be you.

Part 3: Career & job success

Finding a job

It can be difficult to land your first job, but it is also an important milestone in your professional career. Your first job can change the course of your career. For instance, you might discover activities that you genuinely enjoy, which you end up specializing in, or you might find a job niche that opens doors for you.

You can do a few things to make your job search easier. There are many online job sites you can join, both for jobs in specific areas, and also for work from home jobs. If you are in college, do you have internship opportunities? When starting, this is always a good chance to get into the professional world.

Many jobs today require candidates to go through an internship before being considered for trainee or effective positions. Therefore, if you are still an undergraduate student or in the middle of a professional course, it is recommended to start by finding a great internship opportunity.

Exercise networking: it's time to meet people and activate your contacts

The help of a contact can facilitate your first opportunity in the market. The person can recommend you for available jobs in the company where he works or also highlight your profile to other professionals who have open jobs in their work teams.

Another point to consider when looking for your first job is networking. Seeking connections is important at any point of your career, but especially at the beginning. This is because when you meet interesting professionals, in the beginning, they may become good connections in the future.

You can start by connecting with people who are already close to you. People from your course, professors, or other students are a good option if you are in university or a technical course. Also, finding cheap or free courses related to your professional interest in your city may be a good investment at this point. You will not only grow in knowledge, but if you make the most out of that opportunity, you may find valuable contacts with interesting opportunities for your career.

Lastly, attending free events in your area and approaching people for coffee can help you make friends. A conference, seminar, fair, or congress can be an excellent opportunity to stay up to date and to meet new people.

Choosing the right area, preparing yourself for the interview, and putting together a good CV are all important steps in turning an ideal opportunity into a proposal.

Your resume

Considering that a resume is the first step into the world of work, you'll want to carefully consider the details since it's your chance to make a great first impression. If you are building your first resume, lack of experience can be a major concern. Experience is always valuable, even if it appears small, but you can also include other items on your resume.

What should your resume include

Consider your lack of experience an opportunity to learn and start from the ground up in a company instead of a shortcoming. Focus on the things you have regardless of your experience.

- **Personal information**

Include your full name, city, ID number, social media profiles and cell phone numbers. There is no need to enter your marital status or more information.

- **Photo**

Choosing the right picture for your resume is very important. It should show you as a trustworthy and professional person. This does not mean you should not smile in your pictures; a slight smile will make you look energetic and fresh. In any case, it's best to use an official-looking picture with a suit or shirt, preferably with a plain background.

- **Profile**

Briefly describe yourself as "Who I am", in a formal way that is not technical. Include your last level of education, main interests, career objectives, skills, and why you are a good candidate for a company. Four to five lines should be enough.

- **Education**

From the most recent to the oldest, list the levels of your studies chronologically. In addition, list the courses, workshops, etc., you've taken.

- **Achievements**

Highlight any type of recognition, scholarship, award, research, monitoring, publications, volunteering, group participation, award achievements, or any other situation illustrative of your work and leadership style.

- **Professional experience**

For inexperienced candidates, it is the most feared part of their resumes. It's okay if you don't have work experience yet; just remove this section from your profile and complete the rest. Nevertheless, if you have done an internship, some part-time work (delivery person, waiter, etc.), or any volunteering with an association. Those little experiences prove you're responsible and hardworking. In this case, it is good that you include them in this section.

- **Skills**

Take this opportunity to list all the things you're skilled at, like, technological programs, leadership abilities, public speaking, writing, typing, etc. This is the place to show off. Be sure to note which skills and competencies will make you stand out.

- **Languages**

Companies often like to see you speak more than one language since communication with people from other countries who speak a different language is important in this globalized world.

- **References**

If possible, include one or two references who can speak honestly about your abilities. Many people can verify the information on your resume, such as your teachers, classmates, previous employers (if you had any), and others.

How to draw attention to your resume

Since the people who work in personnel selection are usually quite busy, the visual impression your resume makes is essential. To ensure your resume isn't discarded immediately, follow these tips below to get the employer's attention so that your CV will be reviewed.

- Don't use strong colors or hard-to-read fonts. When you submit your resume to a recruiter, make the first meeting friendly and pleasant. They can concentrate on the content if they do not have to make much effort to understand the style.

- Don't have any spelling mistakes. Your ability to write well is directly related to your education level and your ability to express yourself well, which is required in many different positions within organizations. A situation like this would reflect poorly on you and lead to a deduction in points.

- Whether you are preselected will depend on how and what you say. The key is to captivate your reader with short sentences describing your abilities, skills, and other characteristics valuable to the company you want to work for.

- You must express your ideas dynamically, enthusiastically, and positively. It is important to show that you are open to learning and collaborating. Dynamic and motivated employees will always be important within organizations, so project this.

- Your resume should not exceed two pages. Employers will let you know when they need more information, so do not expand too much in your job descriptions.

Not even the most experienced doctor finds it easy to land a new job since job hunting is also a matter of attitude. We must capture information carefully on our resumes because it will be our first chance to make contact with someone who can offer us the opportunity we are looking for. The second chance to make a good impression is in your interview, so prepare for that too.

The job interview

You made it to the interview stage because your resume stood out from the rest. Yet, you shouldn't be overconfident and miss the chance to show your talent and how well you are suited for the position. A job interview can be successful if you listen carefully to the questions asked by the recruiter so that you avoid making mistakes that might make you look bad.

In a selection process, you will usually go through more than one type of interview, so knowing what to expect is important.

Types of interview

Directed interview

This format is used mainly by human resource professionals; it follows a structured pattern of questions. During the job interview, the interviewer asks questions concisely and notes the candidates' answers, which must also be concrete.

Non-directed interview

Typically, these job interviews are conducted by people who are not human resource professionals; they are characterized by their lack of structure and the opportunity for the applicant to take the initiative. The interviewer listens rather than asks more general questions. Through this format, the personality of the interviewee can be further analyzed.

Mixed interview

Combining the two previous types, this method allows the interviewer to ask specific questions and provide opinions and comments to the interviewee. This type of interview is very common.

Panel Interview

In the panel interview, you will be the only one interviewed by a group of interviewers. The objective is to evaluate from different angles if your incorporation will benefit the company and, if it does, in which role you will fit best.

You should behave as you would in a standard interview, answering each separately while smiling and remaining calm. Try to act as if you are a part of a group of acquaintances.

Group interview

One or more interviewers and several interviewees are present here. This type of interview aims to evaluate the candidate's leadership capabilities, interaction with the group, or other behavioral characteristics.

Telephone or online interview

This type of interview aims to make a preselection before going to the personal interview. While this is less nerve-wracking, the disadvantage is that you don't know who is interviewing you, and you can't use your presence to your advantage.

What you need to know to pass your first interview

A job interview can be stressful and nerve-wracking, so being prepared can help control your nerves and increase our chances of success.

- Practice in front of a mirror or with a friend or family member: Doing this before the interview will help you control your non-verbal language during the interview and correct your mistakes. It will also help you organize your ideas and answer the job interview questions more confidently.

- Find out about the company: It is essential to know what it does, what products or services it offers, and its position compared to the competition. You can find out more about the company and how they communicate on their website.

- Dress according to the company environment: If the job is for a bank or consultant, you should wear a suit or formal attire. However, if the job vacancy is at a start-up or a young company, you can dress casually without exceeding the informal boundaries.

- Take a small notebook and a pen: You may need to write down conclusions, questions, or impressions that may arise during the job interview. It is advisable also to bring two or three copies of your resume since you may find yourself with more interviewers than you thought.

- Remember to be punctual on the day of the interview: This is the first step to demonstrating your professionalism and responsibility.

- Control nonverbal language: Avoid playing with objects while interacting with the recruiter, such as pens, and always look him in the eye to demonstrate calm and security.

- Balance your speech: Highlight your abilities, show your desire to learn and work, and avoid bragging or pretending that you already know everything.

- Explain yourself well, answer briefly and coherently: You mustn't interrupt the interviewer and listen carefully to their questions. This will help you answer more accurately.

- Maintain an optimistic, positive and receptive attitude: Ask the recruiter questions at the end of your interview to indicate your interest in the position.

- Do not lie: Recruiters will automatically turn you down if they discover deception or manipulation. Highlight your strengths and qualities only.

Getting a job is not impossible, but it takes commitment and time. Having found the one you're best suited for, it's time to prepare for your first day.

What questions should I expect in my first interview?

"Tell me about yourself."

This type of question is often the first in a job interview. You need to briefly explain who you are (experience, professional profile, training, etc.). The presentation must be brief and focused on the job you desire.

"Why are you looking for a job?"

It would be good to discuss how you need to advance your career or make it complete by gaining experience in other professional fields. If you are unemployed because you were fired, you need to maintain a positive attitude and not dwell on the reasons for the dismissal. Instead, focus on developing a satisfying and interesting career.

"What do you know about us?"

This is probably one of the most common interview questions since you should know about the company before going for an interview.

Getting to know the company is something you should do before you even apply for a job. If not, you will appear uninterested, reducing your chances of getting hired.

"Why do you want to work with us?"

You must prepare an answer that combines your professional development plan with the research you have already done on the company.

"What is of most importance to you in your life?"

You don't have to say that your work is the most important thing to you out of obligation. The best answer would be one that encompasses several aspects of your life. For example: "To me, it's important to strike a balance so that I can enjoy all aspects of life, including spending time with my family and dedicating time to growing professionally."

"What is your experience with the position?"

A perfect profile for the job puts all your points in your favor and shows you are the best candidate. If this is not the case, think about how your experience and technical skills fit into the position in advance.

"What do you like most about the position?"

You must prepare a thoughtful response for these types of questions in a job interview and explain how you are perfect for the position.

"Are you in any other selection process?"

This can be answered honestly. If you are in another selection process, you do not need to mention the company, only the sector and the position you are applying for.

"What would you highlight about yourself as a professional?"

To answer this question in a job interview, you must choose the technical and personal skills you possess that are most relevant to the job. If the position is for a department head, you can highlight your leadership skill, whereas if it's for a technical position, you can emphasize your attention to detail. You should not overlook your qualities as a person, such as honesty, teamwork, responsibility, commitment, and proactivity.

"What is your biggest flaw?"

This is one of the most difficult interview questions to answer. You should pick a minor defect to demonstrate you are aware of it and trying to improve it. Turning a defect into a virtue is already widely seen and may sound false.

"What have you done to broaden your experience?"

Now is the time to demonstrate your proactive approach to your professional development, so please mention any training you have completed related to that goal. Additionally, you may mention personal projects or hobbies that demonstrate qualities such as leadership, organizational skills, etc.

"How are you working in a team?"

It is one of the easiest questions to answer in an interview. Even if you are applying for a position where you work alone, you should emphasize that you enjoy working with others. Use an example to illustrate your point.

"Do you prefer to be feared or liked?"

The question refers to co-workers and employees. Respect might be the right word to use here.

As a professional, I prefer to be respected. In the medium term, fear is not very motivating, so it might not be the best response. Being liked for its own sake is not very productive for a company. Working towards goals and using defined terms is more important.

"What motivation do you need to do a good job?"

These questions in a job interview are common, but avoid mentioning money. Make emphasis on topics like personal satisfaction from problem-solving, improving things, etc.

"When under pressure, how do you cope?"

The key is to be positive in your answer. You may not get the job if you claim that you don't perform well or block yourself.

"What is your greatest professional achievement?"

The best thing is to talk about a project in which you have been involved and has given good results. Do not try to present yourself as the "star" of the project, it is better always to emphasize your participation as part of a work team.

"Tell me about an idea you have had that has been carried out."

If you can provide real facts, you can discuss a change you implemented in your team and how their manner of working allowed you to be more productive.

"What financial aspirations do you have?"

If you want the best answer, you should learn about the salary ranges for that position and about the current situation of the company.

"Where do you see yourself in five years?"

A question like this in a job interview aims to discover how you see yourself developing professionally and if you have a clear vision of where your career will go. You don't need to be very precise since nobody knows what the future holds, but you could discuss how you would like to progress in a particular field or hold positions of more responsibility. Demonstrating a minimum of ambition is the goal.

"What do you do in your free time?"

Use the question to demonstrate how you apply your strengths in your personal life. You play soccer with your friends because you love working together to accomplish a goal. Because you know how to organize a project, you have renovated the house yourself.

"Do you speak any other languages?"

The best way to answer this question well is to do it in the language or languages you mentioned in your resume.

"Why should I hire you and not someone else?"

This is becoming one of the most common questions in recent years, and it is usually asked at the end of a job interview. It's time to remember that your skills, experience, or education fit perfectly with the job description. You can achieve this by making a small list of these favorable points and communicating it to the interviewer. Additionally, remember not to use this question to disqualify the other candidates participating in the selection process, as it could turn against you.

"To finish, do you have any questions?"

When you find out about the company, think of two or three interesting questions you could ask at the end of the job interview. If you have not been answered before (normally, the interviewer introduces the company), choose one and do it at the end of the interview. Even if they don't ask you this question, ask one. It will show your interest in the position.

Small talk recommended topics for the office

Having some topic ideas to share quality time with your co-workers is always a good idea. Some of the best things to talk about are:

- Weekend plans
- Sports
- TV series
- Cooking
- Hobbies in general
- Local news
- Family anecdotes
- Traveling
- Parties, social events, and concerts
- The weather

Stay away from talking about:

- Other people's bodies
- Salary

- Internal critics
- Politics
- Religion
- Gender beliefs
- Personal problems

Going to work

Feeling nervous or anxious is normal when faced with so many new things like new colleagues, bosses, plenty of information, and a new environment that functions differently from your former one. You can have an excellent first day at a new job if you're prepared and consider a few simple things.

Arrive early

It is essential to arrive on time on the first day at work, but it is also a good idea to arrive early. If possible, try to arrive fifteen minutes before your appointment. Plan and use a map app to find the best routes from home to work.

You will not have to study route options if you have a remote job. Still, you will have to get up early, shower, pick an appropriate location (with good lighting and background you will not be ashamed of), and connect punctually or a few seconds before your meeting time.

Ask questions

You will have many questions on your first day at work since you will receive so much information.

Don't hesitate to ask what has not been resolved about your role and obligations, the company, the processes, or the tools you'll be using. It's not a sign of weakness or ignorance but interest.

Get organized

Organizing begins before you leave home and continues once you reach work. Be sure you have all the essentials on hand (computer, pen, notebook, sheets or tablet to record your notes, your glasses, a bottle of water, etc.) and prepare your work area so that your first day on the job is more comfortable and enjoyable.

Relax and enjoy

It is common for a job to create anxiety, especially in environments that have a culture of perfectionism and competition, where results are emphasized. A similar or greater degree of this can also happen on the first day at work.

Be prepared for that anxiety or nerves of starting a new job by getting enough sleep the day before (between seven and eight hours) and giving yourself time to make it to work or the video call.

Relaxation and breathing techniques can also help you feel better if needed.

Your body language

Having the right attitude and body language can help you to present yourself as a person who is open, pleasant, and trustworthy on your first day of work.

For this, you should sit upright, avoid turning your back, look at your conversation partner, and smile when appropriate.

If they invite you to eat, accept

In your first job, the details are important, and mealtime is no exception. You might have brought a salad or some macaroni in a Tupperware or planned to eat at home or your favorite restaurant.

If your colleagues or supervisors ask you to join them for lunch, go along: it is an excellent way to get to know the company, the environment, the relationships, and the people you will live with in a less formal setting.

Learn the language of the organization

All of you will speak one language (or more, if it is a multilingual environment), but each company will also speak its own language. This one is filled with colloquial expressions, abbreviations, acronyms, acronyms, winks, and other elements that can confuse an outsider.

Do not be afraid to ask about them, and try remembering them all (you can write them down). This will make your understanding of meetings and emails and subsequent adaptation easier.

Find out what the professional expectations are

Knowing what is expected of you and your new role will enable you to meet expectations and, if possible, exceed them. On the first day, ask your supervisor about your responsibilities, take notes, and ensure you understand the job's standards.

Turn off your cell phone

Turn off or silence your mobile phone until you need it. Your first day of work can be filled with news, information, presentations, and learning, and you'll need all the concentration you can muster.

Start building your network of contacts

With luck, this will only be the first of many first days at work. Your relationship with your colleagues may be key to your adaptation, resolving doubts, especially in the first weeks, and even developing friendships.

Say thanks

"Rookies" need to be grateful. Thanking those who helped you on the first day of work (and for the opportunity to be a member of the team and company) demonstrates education and respect. This will also prove your positivity and willingness to contribute to the company.

Clothes

To begin with, there is no set rule for what constitutes a professional look since the work environment determines the code of style. You should consider the image of the company, the size, the average age of your colleagues, and the role you play. The style of the interviewers you saw during the selection process can be useful as a guide.

Casual

You can dress casually if you work in an informal environment without direct contact with clients. Sometimes even companies with formal dress codes offer casual Fridays so that you can be comfortable and sporty. However, a casual office appearance does not mean sloppy, or looking like you don't' care about the job. Stay away from slippery dresses, shorts, and tops with spaghetti straps. You can wear sneakers with jeans in this style. Just not ripped jeans.

Smart Casual

This look is trendy in young companies with young employees and a professional attitude. The basis for this style is blazers and shirts without ties, pastel-colored blouses and palazzo or cigarette pants, and knee-length dresses. Sporty looks and more elegant elements combine in the smart casual dress code. All in all, it's a professional yet comfortable outfit that will make you appear friendly without losing credibility.

Business casual

As it stands, this dress code has a formal office look. In addition to professionalism, comfort and accessories also play a part. It's the ideal look for structured businesses, especially for meetings or lunches with clients. A suit is appropriate for men, but women can choose soft or straight-cut skirts or trousers in the version without a tie. Pastel shades and soft colors are perfect.

Business

This is the most important part of any office wardrobe. Even if you are not part of a large corporation, consider it the best choice for conferences, meetings, and presentations. Jacket and tie for him, blue, gray or beige, suit jacket and pants or jacket for her. Closed shoes, heels, but not more than 10 cm.

How to get a promotion

A career promotion is one of a professional's most important goals. It represents an improvement in your career and offers the chance to keep advancing. As a result, it is recognition for your commitment.

Promotions are an excellent indicator of career growth. Promotion is also highly motivating for any employee since it represents professional advancement and benefits one's quality of life - but only if that is one of your life goals. Promotion signifies recognition of service, loyalty, and professionalism. It is also proof that you are valued by the company you work for. Additionally, it represents the challenge of growing on a personal and professional level to fulfill your new position's responsibilities. You need to know where you are in your career and understand what you lack to reach the next level.

Promotions allow the company to fill specific positions with professionals familiar with them.

Promoting you, a professional with experience and knowledge of the company, its policies, and culture, automatically eliminates the need to select and train new employees.

You can be promoted without changing your position in the organization chart. Changing your role and responsibilities is part of a job-level promotion; however, this doesn't entail moving offices or changing jobs. Instead, it is an adjustment to your job description. Sometimes, you will need to seek internal advice to complete this process. You can find out what promotions are available by contacting Human Resources. Remember that promotions are not always about changing positions.

Which types of promotions are there?

It can be job rotations, transfers, or promotions. All these mean different things, and we usually get confused between these different types of movements. A job rotation may imply a change in your work description without new benefits, while transfers can include experiencing a change of headquarters or department. However, you will continue to perform the same tasks wherever you are assigned.

When it comes to promotions, there are two main types you can aspire to. You can earn a promotion through seniority. This means that promotions are based on years of service. You can also earn a promotion by merit. This means they can be faster to get and will depend on your performance.

How Do I Get a Promotion at Work?

Every company has its own promotions, but there are some common factors that make you a good candidate. It usually starts with a need. Some functions are not covered, so a gap opens up. Internal changes and upcoming projects also lead to these gaps.

Although different scenarios can generate the possibility of promotion, experts in the field of human talent agree that the following qualities define a successful candidate for promotion:

- Productivity: Being able to carry out and promote the company's projects is key. Employees with vision, who are goal-oriented, and take plans to the next level, are the right candidates.
- Leadership: Being a leader means not being afraid to create and execute ideas independently.

- Availability: Promotions involve increased responsibilities and tasks. To accomplish this, you must be an employee with enough time to tackle the challenges.

- Productivity: One of the key points. As long as you represent benefits and growth for the company, you will be eligible for a job promotion.

You can make getting a promotion easier if you consider some factors.

- Stand out: The best way to make yourself eligible for additional responsibilities is to do the ones you have now very well. You'll demonstrate that you're capable and ready for the next step.

- Make sure you are qualified: The most important step is preparing for your desired position. Spend some time studying the position and the new areas. Take courses, learn a language and improve your professional skills.

- Talk to your superior: Discussing your interest in a promotion is a great way to be considered. Make your superiors aware of your desire for more responsibility.

- Observe: This task is simple but crucial. You can become the solution if you recognize the needs of the business.

- Know the methods to get recognised and ear-marked for promotion: To ascend, you must know what to do. Learn what a promotion candidate's profile looks like.

- Find out if you want the promotion: Make sure you want those responsibilities. Understand what the promotion entails before applying for it.

- Make yourself known: Popularity is key because this likable and friendly behavior makes room for leadership.

- Have a plan: You need to draw up an action plan. Moving forward and knowing what steps you need to take is a must.

When it comes to job promotion, there are no shortcuts. Professional accomplishment results from your time and disposition and, most importantly, from your preparation. You have to be fully trained and dedicated to it. As a result, do not rule out the possibility of training, gaining experience, and growing professionally.

Working from home

There are many benefits of working from home, but it's a lifestyle that requires self-discipline if you want to sustain it into the future. Even if you're glued to the computer all day, you can fool yourself into thinking something is work that isn't. Getting distracted by social media isn't working! By following these steps, you can create a helpful physical and mental environment for being productive.

Establish a routine (or several)

For your body and brain to know when to work and rest, you must maintain a certain amount of regularity in your daily routine. Schedule your day according to your individual needs and include work time, rest time, leisure time, and exercise time. Find a routine and schedule that works for you by experimenting with different options.

Plan your daily schedule

Choosing what to do is the most difficult part. You must know what you will be doing each day.

If possible, spend five minutes before going to bed writing down what you will do the next day. Knowing what you will do the next day before you go to bed will help you sleep better and wake up with clear ideas.

The process of planning each day is, of course, based on your weekly review of your projects and tasks. You will need to take a broader view of your goals and responsibilities every few months.

Work on your TMIs first

You must identify the Most Important Tasks(TMIs) when defining your daily action plan, that is, those tasks you must complete as soon as possible since they will bring you closer to completing projects and achieving goals.

Avoid distractions

Every day, you should set aside a few moments to handle email, phone calls, access social networks, read blogs, etc. Then turn them off, and disable your notifications to stop you being distracted while you're working.

You can go a step; further and take the apps of your phone too. There are some software programs you can install on your computer that will also track the time you spend on websites.

Remember why you do what you do

With time, you will likely lose perspective and motivation to keep working hard. Motivating yourself is vital. You can use sticky notes, posters, and reminders to help you remember your values and goals at work. Keep a visual system that reminds you daily why you do what you do, where you are, and where you want to go.

Locate alternative workplaces

As you probably already know, working at home every day is exhausting. Even if your workplace is comfortable, sitting in the same place all day can become tiresome, especially if you do not interact with others. If you're going to a cafe, look for one with WiFi, good coffee, friendly people, and little noise. You can talk to someone about anything and do tasks that don't require as much concentration there; you'll find it refreshing.

Prepare a comfortable workspace

You should reserve an area where you work exclusively and not use other parts of the house for work, like the bed or the couch in front of the TV. Create clear boundaries between work and personal life.

Maintain a clean and tidy work surface where you can easily work. Make sure your workspace is pleasant. You'll spend many hours there, so make sure you get a comfortable chair that allows you to maintain good posture.

Make sure the room is well acclimatized. Don't hesitate; excessive heat or cold will make your workday miserable. Lighting is also crucial. Consider working in a place with good natural light, avoid reflections on the computer screen, and use a cold white light lamp (it won't generate heat) if you work at night.

Having a culture of workplace wellness (in our home offices or regular offices) will allow us to integrate health into our daily routine. Having a clear mind, preventing illness, coming up with better ideas, being more efficient, and dealing with work situations more effectively are some of the changes we will see.

Home office basics

The ten essential elements that your "home office" should have.

1) Computer

A laptop is a good idea if your work requires you to travel frequently. However, getting a desktop computer might make more sense if you don't need to move. Desktop computers can be built to be faster and more powerful than laptops.

2) Internet connection

You need to be connected to the internet. For better performance, a broadband connection is recommended. The signal must be stable and strong, so you can do your work without difficulty. Be sure to hire a reputable service provider.

3) Peripherals

The list includes; a monitor, keyboard, mouse, printer, scanner, webcam, and headphones. A widescreen monitor is extremely important (you can even have two monitors, depending on your work).

4) Phone / Smartphone

You will find it very useful to always have your smartphone and landline when you work from home. Often overlooked, this is no small detail. Keep in mind that they complement VoIP tools.

5) Furniture

You will need a desk, a chair, even a cabinet or shelf for filing documents, books, or other items. They should be functional and adaptable to your needs. It is important to have an ergonomic desk and chair for good posture during working hours. In addition, modern design has led to furniture that appears like "household furniture" that is very comfortable, useful, and functional. If you look carefully, you can design a home that looks like a warm and inviting office while simultaneously being functional for you to work at your own pace.

6) Good lighting

The lighting in your office should be perfect, if possible, natural. You can prevent headaches, eyestrain, and even poor posture due to not being able to see the screen clearly.

7) Memos / Notepads

Whatever your specialty, memos, and notebooks are useful for putting together lists or outlines, downloading ideas, and more. Various materials and designs are available to suit all tastes and are essential for a home office.

8) Software

Instant messaging, email, voice-over IP applications, and automatic backup programs are also helpful. You can also use the online resources to edit documents, share files, manage projects, and do thousands of other things.

9) Office supplies

The supplies include clips, staplers, highlighters, folders, files, scissors, and envelopes. Create a list of everything you need daily and what else you might need. Basic office supplies are an excellent idea to keep on hand.

10) Your personal touch

You need to make your home office "your real home office". Put a picture of where you want to go on vacation, a desk clock, a mini-poster of your favorite doll, etc. It should reflect your style. Have you given it any thought?

Part 4: Entrepreneurship & money

Money management

Financial stability is very important as we develop into adults. This is true if you are a student, an employee, or want to become an entrepreneur. In an economy as unpredictable as today's, knowing how to manage the money we have right now is of utmost importance. Even though we know it is not easy to plan expenses and save enough to build wealth, especially for those who want to start their own business.

Money in our everyday life assumes different forms: credits, taxes, debt, investments, and assets. But before we go into the different areas of your financial world, let's review some basic things to keep in mind when managing money.

The basics of managing money

Write down your fixed expenses

Keeping track of fixed expenses is essential to determine how much income is left over to invest, save or allocate to rest and leisure each month. You must also be aware of the fixed expenses of your business, such as rent and production costs.

Set aside at least 10% of your income

Make sure to reserve at least 10% of your income for investing before paying fixed expenses. This is not just about saving money until you can spend it on something extra. It's also about applying those savings so that they will earn interest and become a significant asset in the future.

Pay off your debts as soon as possible.

As soon as you have received a loan in your name, you may want to consider paying more installments simultaneously to reduce the length of the contract and, of course, interest. If you have multiple loans or credit card debit, pay off the loan with the highest interest rate first.

Learn to invest

You can protect your money by investing, so you don't waste it on unnecessary things. But when we use the word "investment". An investment can be buying some stock in the S&P 500, or it can be buying an online course to increase your knowledge and skills, so you have the tools to generate more income for yourself in the future.

About 10 years ago I invested $1997 in an online course to teach me how to start a mobile app business, without needing to have any mobile app programming skills. That investment paid itself back in revenue many times over.

In most cases, clothes and shoes, luxury holidays and parties are not an investment. We've all read the story of successful athletes or lottery prize winners who blow through millions of dollars over a few months or years, without investing in anything, and end up penniless.

Set limits on variable expenses

Anything that is not a fixed expense is a variable expense.

In other words, an expense can, in principle, be postponed. Nevertheless, in practice, people do not want to stop depriving themselves of small pleasures, like going out with friends, going on a trip, or buying a gift that is not indispensable.

The best thing you can do in these cases is to set a limit. Make sure you set aside a small amount of money for your leisure activities.

Use financial management tools

Several financial management programs and applications are available if you aren't comfortable working with spreadsheets and need a simpler way of controlling your expenses.

They may allow you to upload receipts of credit card payments, track bank transactions, and even insert bill payment reminders. As a result, you are in control of everything that enters and leaves your account. Late fees and interest will no longer surprise you. Try out a few popular apps on the app store.

Look for alternative sources of income

These days, you can earn money by doing many different things from the comfort of your own home. Most of these alternative sources of income only require a computer, internet, and some time. From freelancing to entrepreneurship, there are a ton of options out there for people who want to earn passive income or add extra revenue to their monthly income.

Define an average budget

To avoid unpleasant surprises, take an average of your income from the past few months and identify the periods when you earn more or less, as well as the impact of seasonality on your sales, such as holiday periods, high season, and low season.

You should be able to pay your fixed expenses with your minimum income. In the months of high billing, when you earn more than the average for the year, invest or save your surplus so that you are prepared for the months of low billing.

Buy smartly

Previously, it was explained that how you spend your money impacts your economic well-being.

You can improve your financial reality by joining reward programs, comparing prices on the internet, and buying second-hand products.

Create an emergency fund

Many people spend most of their income, so their financial situation is fragile when an emergency occurs. Aside from your 10% reserve of income for investing, it is important to reserve an additional percentage in case of emergencies.

There is a difference between this fund and the previous one since money in this fund must be liquid and easy to move. On the other hand, investments do not have these characteristics, which is why it is important to distinguish the investment fund from the emergency fund.

The amount of this fund is usually less than the investment fund, but you must also consider it since it can help you make sure you are prepared for anything. In terms of money management, saving and controlling money is only one part. The other is to become more efficient by generating it.

In the end, investing more means earning more, which means more money to buy something important or improve your business.

Investing

Fear is usually one of the common denominators many savers have when deciding to make their money grow. The fear of losing what has been gained is always there. For this reason, it is challenging to invest for the first time. Investments need to be after a lot of thought and research. However, there are a few tips to keep in mind when investing for the first time.

Set an amount to invest initially

The first thing that should be done is to determine what assets you have available for investment. To attain this goal, experts always recommend dedicating to the investment world the income you don't need to live (which does not go to your emergency fund).

Set investment goals

Once you consider your risk profile and the money you want to invest, you can set investment goals. Where do you want to go? What are the goals you have set for yourself? Usually, these investment objectives tend to have a lot to do with the savings we want to generate for retirement, with the goal of maintaining our purchasing power.

The importance of diversification

Regardless of your profile as an investor, it is always important to diversify among the assets to invest. It is known as "not putting all your eggs in the same basket, but different ones". Thus, the possibility that a specific asset's bad behavior harms your portfolio's performance is prevented.

Assets vs. liability

In financial language, there are many specialized terms that, to the general public less familiar with such matters, may present serious challenges when trying to understand the concepts they refer to. A good example is how poorly we usually understand the difference between "assets" and "liabilities". An asset can be viewed in a very elementary manner as a product or good that generates income for its owner. On the other hand, a liability is anything that causes us expense.

Holding dividend generating shares of a company is an good example of an asset since the shares generate income, often through quarterly, semi-annual or annual dividends. It's also accumulating possible revaluations in the share price.

One of the most well-known liabilities is buying a car. Almost everyone makes a car purchase at least once during their lifetime. And, of course, there is a saying that says, "You lose money the second you leave the dealership". This is a genuine truth since the expenses it produces, and its depreciation increases with its age.

However, in the world of financial markets and investments, nothing is black or white. The future market circumstances that determine whether or not you made the right decision. That's why it is important to remember that if the investment you are going to make "keeps you awake at night", don't do it. And always seek professional advice before investing.

Entrepreneurship

Entrepreneurship and starting your own business is very different from managing or working for a company. As an entrepreneur, your goal is to take the initiative and make a decision to pursue a business venture that allows you to enter the market, either by manufacturing a product or by providing a service.

The best way I've seen entrepreneurs succeed is to follow the market. Research what people are already buying and make a better version of it. And there is a very accessible way to figure this out. It's called the internet. Many of us now work online - in addition to our traditional jobs - because the web has changed the nature of work. Through online business, there are an unlimited number of ways to earn income, whether passive or active.

Passive income differs from active income mainly by whether or not you need to be involved when the income is generated. For example, I wrote this book once. But it has bene sold many times.

Once you create the asset, you don't have to do a lot extra to generate revenue from it. Your money increases passively. However, if you're a freelance web designer, then you need to turn on your computer and make new websites every day to get paid.

Online side hustles

You can generate passive income online in many ways. By creating something (a blog, an e-book, online course, print on demand t-shirts, subscription service, mobile apps, a clothing line or an online store), you can generate passive income even when you are not working.

Create an online course

Selling online courses is among the best ways to earn passive income. There are a number of course hosting platforms out there who will host all your videos, payments and student management for a very small fee. Your main responsibilities are to create an online course that people are interested in and would buy, and then secondly, let people know the course exists by sharing tips and fun videos about it on social media - which could be anything from Facebook and Instagram to Tiktok and Youtube.

Online course prices can range in value from $1 to $2000 and beyond! If you add coaching to your courses, you can charge up to $25,000 per person per year depending on your niche and experience.

Sell physical products online

Many digital nomads are entrepreneurs who travel around the world and make money from their laptop. It sounds a little crazy but it works as I've done this too. One of the most popular business types for nomads is ecommerce. That's selling physical products (that you never see or touch!) online, usually through websites like Amazon or Shopify. If you pick the right products, this can be very lucrative. You can also do drop-shipping. The idea is that someone buys a product on your website, and you then order the product to be shipped directly from the producer to the customer. You are a sort of online middleman. If either option sounds interesting, I'd suggest you watch some of the many videos on youtube on this topic.

Become a freelancer

Many online businesses these days hire people from all over the world to work from home and help them grow their businesses.

Great at Tiktok? Cool. Offer to help local businesses grow their following and sales on Tiktok. Great at writing copy? You can get hired as an email or sales page copywriter. Love video editing? Get a freelancing job editing videos for virtual summits, promotions or repurposing youtube videos into reels and Tiktiks.

Love social media?

Perfect. Build up your profile on your platform of choice and you could be an influencer, with brands paying you to share their product online. You'll find tons of examples of this on all the social media platforms.

Sell the things you no longer need

Why not take advantage of Marie Kondo's tips for earning passive income? Get rid of items that no longer serve you and sell them to generate more income. You'd be surprised how many people are willing to buy second-hand books, clothes, and kitchen utensils. This is a fun way to tidy up your house and generate some extra income.

Get paid for sponsored posts on social media

More and more businesses are paying social media accounts to promote their products and services through influencer marketing. Whether you're interested in travel, fashion, beauty, home decor, or wacky dog haircuts, there's a niche for you.

As the most known platforms allow you to create fan pages for just about anything, social media sponsored posts are a great way to earn money.

You don't need to start selling something; building an audience is more important. Companies will offer you their products so you can market them or speak well of them (for a commission or a single payment). Also, don't forget to use hashtags to gain more exposure and reach a larger audience.

Create your own blog

You can make passive income online by creating your blog. Through affiliate links, advertising, courses, sponsored posts, products, book deals, and more, blogging has enabled countless bloggers and entrepreneurs to earn passive income.

It indeed takes time to build a successful blog. However, since it's a great way to earn a passive income, it may be worth the effort.

Join affiliate marketing

It's good to know that almost every big brand has an affiliate program. For instance, some brands' affiliate programs pay up to $2,000 per referral. Other online retailers, however, provide referral bonuses of just 10%. Therefore, you must research the best affiliate programs before beginning your career. You can generate affiliate commissions through blogging without spending any money on ads.

Create a print-on-demand store

Taking advantage of today's e-commerce boom can be a great way to make passive income if you are an accomplished designer. You can sell custom graphics on products like clothing, mugs, banners, phone cases, bags, and more with print-on-demand. What's great about this is that you can create your products and build a brand. Amazon has a print on demand t-shirt program called Merch by Amazon. There are other websites there too like Teespring and Printful.

Write an eBook

The ebook has remained a popular content medium since it became all the rage in 2010. If you are a natural writer, you can earn passive income by writing an ebook.

Create an app

Without a doubt, this is one of the most original ideas on how to generate passive income. You can create applications that generate passive income online as a programmer or developer. You can generate assets by charging a fee to people who purchase your app or make your app free and monetize your passive work with ads. The good news is you also don't need to be a programmer. You can outsource the programming work overseas on a platform like Upwork.

Create YouTube videos

YouTube is a great way to generate passive income online. You can make quite a lot with YouTube, from sponsored videos to banner ads. The key to creating a successful YouTube channel is consistently creating content for a few months.

With time, you'll see that all your efforts are worthwhile, and you'll really enjoy passive income.

Passive income offers a large number of benefits over costs. And the most important thing is that it is not necessary to give up your job to earn extra income if you enjoy what you do.

Whether you want to start by writing an e-book, investing in stocks, or creating content to sell on-demand, consider how much time you can spend earning passive income. After that, getting started is the only thing left to do.

Paying taxes

Taxes are something you'll encounter as you become an adult and start earning your own money. Doing your taxes can be a little daunting for someone without prior experience.

What are taxes, and why do we need them?

Every country has public services such as public education, postal services, law enforcement, health care, and we invest in innovation and technology. People and institutions that provide these public services must, of course, be paid. Citizens pay for those services indirectly through taxes. In the USA, these public services are offered at the state and federal levels. Citizens are taxed both at the state and federal levels.

USA taxes

In the simplest terms, most taxes can be divided into three categories: taxes on your earnings, purchases, and assets. You need to know how taxes work and how they are calculated in order to understand them. You must also determine your taxable income, distinguishing between tax deductions and tax credits. Understanding how taxes work for businesses and investors differently from how they do for everyday taxpayers is vital. As a result of incorporating these concepts, it will be easier for you to understand how to file a tax return and how to put together a tax plan that works for you.

Taxes on what you earn

The US tax system is set up in such a way that everyone pays their fair share of taxes. In other words, based on your income and the amount you receive, you have to pay taxes on a certain percentage. That can't be done by having a tax rate that is the same for everyone; that would not be fair. For example, if someone earns $200,000 a year and pays 30% in taxes, they would still have $140,000 left over, enough to enjoy a nice lifestyle. On the other hand, if someone earns $40,000 and then they have to pay 30% in taxes, then they only have $28,000 left over, which is barely enough to make ends meet.

As a result, instead of having a flat tax rate in the United States that applies to everyone, we have what is known as a progressive tax system, in which you pay higher tax rates as your income increases. This makes the system a little more equitable since it gives people with lower incomes a tax advantage to make a comeback. The tax rates are summarized as tax brackets.

In 2022, as a single taxpayer, you will pay a 10% tax rate on your first $10,275 taxable income, then 12% on your next $10,276 to $41,775 taxable income and so on. And remember, you are taxed progressively. So, for example, if you make $100,000, even though that puts you in the 24% tax bracket, you wouldn't pay a flat 24% tax rate. Instead, you would only be taxed 24% percent on the income you made between $89,076 and $100,000, which in this case means only $10,924 would be taxed at the 24% tax rate, and the rest would be taxed at the other tax rates. These numbers usually change each year, so make sure to check the latest numbers online

- **Calculating taxes on what you earn.**

The amount of taxes you owe is determined by your taxable income, which is distinct from what you make overall. You can calculate your taxable income by subtracting your tax deductions. By default, all American taxpayers are given a standard deduction. The amount of your standard deduction depends on your filing status, whether you are filing single, married jointly, married separately, or filing head of household. The numbers also change each year, so check the current numbers in your area.

You can calculate your taxes by taking your total income minus all your qualified deductions to determine your taxable income. Once this is done, you will have a tentative tax owed since tax credits must also be accounted for before deciding your final tax owed.

- **Tax deductions vs. tax credits**

Understanding the differences between the two is important. In the example above, it was demonstrated how tax deductions help reduce taxable income. Tax credits, however, are applied to your tax liability. For example, if you earned $100,000 in income, and then deducted $25,000 from that, you have a $75,000 taxable income, and you may owe $10,000 in taxes. In that case, if they had a tax credit of $3,000, it would be applied to their tax liability, and they would pay only $7,000 in taxes after the credit was applied.

Generally, tax credits provide a stronger benefit than tax deductions, but you shouldn't seek as many deductions or credits as possible; rather, you should know what is available and useful for your particular situation.

· **The role of entrepreneurship and real estate**

While taxes are a way to pay for government services internally and externally, it seems that citizens simply paying taxes and governments providing services aren't enough to build and sustain a thriving economy.

Certain tax benefits are only available to certain people, such as tax incentives for investors and business owners. This kind of economy has many quality jobs available so that people can earn a living. Also, a thriving economy is one where people have quality and affordable living places. Two types of people are essential to provide these things: entrepreneurs and real estate investors.

The government gives tax breaks to entrepreneurs and real estate investors to encourage job creation and housing. These tax breaks cover travel expenses, entertainment expenses, clothing expenses, vehicle expenses, job tax credits, and so on.

There are two types of earnings for tax purposes, earned and unearned. Earned income is money that you receive from actively working. Wages, salaries, tips, self-employment income, etc., are examples of earned income. In contrast, unearned income is something you receive without actively working. For example, real estate income, interest income, stock dividends, or any other dividend would be examples of this.

The average person pays more taxes on earned income, especially W-2 income, since these are subject to payroll taxes, which include Medicare and Social Security payments, but usually, the employer covers half.

However, if you are self-employed, you are responsible for all payroll taxes, also known as self-employment taxes. Because of this, unearned income is often the best type of income for tax purposes because you don't have to pay payroll taxes or even income taxes on certain types of unearned income, like the sale of assets or qualified dividends.

It takes a lot of time and hard work to get to the stage in life where you can make investments that turn into unearned income, but the sooner you start, the better.

- **How to build an income tax plan.**

A tax planning strategy involves proactively evaluating how to optimize your taxes to give you the desired result, which could be reducing your overall tax liability, aggressively investing in your business, or planning and saving for retirement. To do so successfully, follow these steps.

1. Understand your tax bracket

Tax plans are probably unnecessary if you do not make much money or do not pay much in taxes. If you are, you should understand where you are and how you can save taxes by shifting tax brackets.

2. Understand tax deductions and tax credits

To meet your overall goals, you can even use online calculators to determine what tax deductions and credits you qualify for.

3. Choose your tax strategy

To maximize your tax situation, you can do many things. Examples include maximizing deductions, optimizing your legal entity structure, planning for retirement, and using insurance strategies. Other advanced tax planning strategies such as investing in real estate or oil and gas may also suit your situation. It's important to stick to just one solid strategy, especially if you have little taxable income.

4. Implement your plan

Once you have selected the tax strategies that best meet your goals, you must implement your plan. This means you may need to set up different retirement or health savings accounts. You may also need to start making investments such as investing in real estate or investing in oil, and gas or even budgeting business expenses for the year and so on.

Taxes on What You Buy

When you purchase something in the USA, various taxes are applied. The price you pay will vary depending on many factors, such as the product you buy, the production process, and the state in which you are located.

- Sales Taxes

A sales tax is a consumption tax on retail sales of goods and services. You have likely seen the sales tax printed at the bottom of your store receipts if you live in the U.S. The U.S. is one of the few nations that use traditional retail sales taxes to raise revenue. All U.S. states collect state and local sales taxes except for Alaska, Delaware, Montana, New Hampshire, and Oregon.

Gross Receipts Taxes

In a gross receipts tax (GRT), the amount of the company's gross sales is taxed, whether profitable or not, without deducting any business expenses. GRTs are harmful to startups, which suffer losses in the early years, and businesses with long production chains.

- Value-Added Taxes

Value Added Taxes (VAT) are consumption taxes assessed on the value added during each production stage. Each business along the production chain pays a VAT on the value of the produced good/service at that stage, with the previous VAT paid for the good/service being deductible at each step. The final customer has to pay VAT without deducting the previously paid VAT. This is a tax on final consumption.

- Excise Taxes

In addition to the broad consumption tax, excise taxes are taxes imposed on specific goods or activities, accounting for a relatively small portion of total tax revenue.

Cigarettes, alcohol, soda, gasoline, and betting are examples of excise taxes. Taxes on excise can be used as "sin" taxes to offset harmful side effects or consequences not reflected in the cost of a product.

Taxes on Things You Own (Property Taxes)

Immovable property taxes are primarily levied on land and buildings and are an important source of revenue for U.S. governments. Property taxes account for more than 30 percent of state and local tax collections in the U.S and over 70 percent of local tax collections. Governments need property tax revenue to support public services, such as schools, roads, police and fire departments, and emergency medical services. In addition to residential property taxes on land and structures, known as "real" property taxes, many states also tax "tangible personal property" (TPP), such as vehicles and equipment owned by individuals and businesses. Taxes on tangible personal property tend to be more problematic since they are less stable, neutral, and transparent.

- Tangible Personal Property (TPP)

Tangible personal property (TPP) includes items that can be moved or touched, such as business equipment, machinery, inventory, furniture, and automobiles. Taxes on TPP account for a small percentage of total state and local tax collections. Their complexity creates high compliance costs. They also favor some industries over others by being nonneutral, distorting investment decisions.

- Estate and Inheritance Taxes

Upon a person's death, both estate and inheritance taxes are imposed. The estate itself pays taxes on estates before assets are distributed to heirs, but the heir pays taxes on inheritance. Both taxes are typically paired with a "gift tax," so they cannot be avoided by transferring property before death.

- Wealth Taxes

Generally, a wealth tax is imposed on an individual's net worth (assets fewer than liabilities) over a certain year's threshold. Under a wealth tax of 5 percent, an individual with wealth above $1 million would have to pay $50,000 in taxes. An individual with a wealth of $2.5 million and a debt of $500,000 would have a net worth of $2 million.

UK taxes

As with any country, the United Kingdom has a fully-integrated Tax System to manage government spending and sustain the country's development.

PAYE tax

The term PAYE refers to pay as you earn. Employees usually pay tax through PAYE. PAYE ensures that amounts owed over a year are collected evenly on each payday. Whenever you receive a salary, your employer deducts Income Tax (IT), Pay Related Social Insurance (PRSI), and Universal Social Charge (USC). Then they send the amount deducted to Revenue. It is possible to reduce the amount of taxes you pay by taking advantage of tax credits, tax reliefs, and exemptions. Scottish citizens must contribute 10% to the Scottish government.

Consumption taxes

The value-added tax (VAT) has different tax rates. There is a standard rate of 20% and a reduced rate of 5%. This number may change each year. These rates apply to certain categories of goods and services and to fuel and energy facilities. Some basic products, such as books, clothing, footwear, and some types of food, have a 0% tax rate.

How do I calculate taxes?

As a general rule, the tax is not due if the salary does not exceed £10,600. This number may change each year.

Withholding claim

You may be able to get a refund of some of the withheld taxes if you stop working before the end of a fiscal year. However, you have up to four years to apply for the money, and to do so, you must fill out one of the following forms: P45, P50, Q60, P85, P800.

Credit score

The term "credit score" in the USA refers to a range of scores from 300 to 850 based on the probability that a person will pay back their debt on time. Because the U.S. economy is based on credit, a person's credit score is one of the most important data. Although there are several types of credit scores, FICO (for Fair Isaac Corporation) is the one most commonly used. The report is from a credit report created by one of the three main credit bureaus, Equifax, Experian, and TransUnion.

How to improve credit score

You can achieve a good credit score by buying on credit and paying off the credit on time.

You can build your credit history by getting a credit card, making small purchases with it, and paying them off in full or leaving a small balance of less than 30% of your monthly credit limit.

Credit cards and loans are the main types of financial products that improve credit scores. Credit history is not affected by debit or prepaid cards, nor the amount of money in a bank account.

Old accounts are much more important to improving your credit rating than recent ones. In addition, keeping the balance on old credit cards below 30% of the credit limit helps increase your FICO score. In light of this, closing or leaving inactive old accounts is not recommended.

If you do not pay a debt on time, going through repossession by a collection agency, bankruptcy, and other financial problems hurt your credit score and stay on your credit record for seven years. If that period has passed, they do not affect the FICO either for or against.

Debt

There are many different reasons why people end up in debt. The path and circumstances that make you feel you have lost control of what you owe can be endless, from medical emergencies leading to thousands of dollars in medical bills to spending your way into debt. In either case, you must decide to cancel your debts.

Getting out of debt and staying out of debt requires a plan. As long as we follow some guidelines, we can prepare for the worst while hoping for the best. Structure and plans help us keep moving in the right direction. If you lose track of where you are going, a plan will help you get back on track.

While in college, some students may be nervous about borrowing student loans for the first time, opting instead to use their credit cards to assist in paying for personal and educational expenses. You might also consider getting into large loans, such as car buying. Although there are differences between these options, all are forms of borrowing. Therefore, when it comes to canceling debt, it is best to know what to prioritize at the point of paying off debt so that you can calculate your financial decisions accordingly.

When canceling debt, you can do it by prioritizing the amount owed or the interest rate. Whatever payoff method you choose, the most important thing is that you are consistent and organized.

By amount owed.

Following this method, you would list your debts, starting with the smallest and working your way up to the biggest debt.

For example:

- Credit Card #1 – $150 (19% Interest)

- Credit Card #2 – $1,000 (17.5 % Interest)

- Vehicle #1 Loan – $7,000 (4.21% Interest)

- Credit Card #3 – $8,800 (17% Interest)

- Credit Card #4 – $14,000 (18% Interest)

- Vehicle #2 Loan – $27,000 (4% Interest)

- Student Loans – $90,000 (7% Interest)

When all your debts are reorganized, you pay the minimum payments except for the smallest payments. It's important to prioritize paying off the lowest debt as soon as possible. After the lowest debt is paid off, move on to the next one until all the debt is paid off.

By interest rate

As far as paying off debt is concerned, this method makes more sense mathematically than any other. It is aimed at paying off debt quickly but requires a lot of discipline. You may find it works best if you are dedicated and focused.

To begin with, list out all your debts in order of interest rate. List your debts, starting with the largest interest rate and going down to the smallest.

Following the previous example:

- Credit Card #1 – $150 (19% Interest)

- Credit Card #4 – $14,000 (18% Interest)

- Credit Card #2 – $1,000 (17.5 % Interest)

- Credit Card #3 – $8,800 (17% Interest)

- Student Loans – $90,000 (7% Interest)

- Vehicle #1 Loan – $7,000 (4.21% Interest)

- Vehicle #2 Loan – $27,000 (4% Interest)

When the debts are listed, it's time to pay the minimum payments on all but the one with the highest interest rate. As with the last method, pay off the highest interest rate debt as quickly as possible. Once you pay off the highest interest rate debt, move on to the next one until you have paid off all the debt.

In addition to being the fastest way to pay off debt, this method reduces the amount of debt added to other loans by eliminating high-interest rates first. Ultimately, this will save you money in the long run. On the other hand, as you don't always see immediate "wins", you need to be focused and committed in order to succeed.

To choose the right system, you need to be honest with yourself. It is best to start with the system based on the amount owed if you are unsure which one would work best for you.

Ultimately, it doesn't matter what method you choose as long as you stick to it. In the end, it wouldn't matter which plan you chose if you quit halfway through. Sticking with it is more important than which plan you follow.

Savings

Now that we have addressed these aspects of your economy, it is time to put some order into your savings decisions. It is necessary to be aware of what you owe and what you own before you can start saving every month. It means you should look at every dollar you earn and spend, including the interest you pay on your credit card balance, monthly bills, taxes, and savings contributions.

Saving money is not just about saving for its own sake; it is also about saving money to achieve one's dreams. There is a big difference.

There is no doubt that one of the best ways to save money is to set a goal that you can achieve. Start by asking yourself what you are saving for. Is it to get married, go on a vacation, or save for retirement? Then you need to calculate roughly how much money you will need and how long it will take you to save that money. It is a good idea to divide objectives into short-term and long-term goals and establish each separately.

Short-term goals (1 to 3 years)

- Emergency fund (have money to support yourself for a few months, just in case)
- Vacations
- Down payment on a new car

Long-term goals (4 years or more)

- Down payment on a house, remodel, or big move
- Quality education for your children
- Retirement contributions

Setting an immediate goal like getting a new smartphone or holiday gifts can prevent you from getting stuck. Reaching smaller savings goals and enjoying the reward you've saved for can give you a psychological boost that makes saving more rewarding and strengthens the habit of saving.

Buying a house

The purchase of a house is a big event in anyone's life. The sense of achievement you get when you own your home can be very satisfying.

However, not everything about purchasing a house is simple, so you should consider your situation carefully. In most cases, buying a house can create some challenges, such as less freedom of movement and quite often a substantial amount of debt, which you need to ensure that you can afford.

Once you decide to purchase a house, these are usually the steps you should take:

1. Adjust your finances: You must know exactly how much money you have saved and how much you can save in the near future

2. Decide your budget: Once you know this number, you can direct your search to more realistic options so that you don't face problems in the future. By keeping this in mind, you can ensure that you are not distracted by

properties that may interest you but are out of your reach.

3. Make sure you have a real estate agent: During the process, you'll need to be guided by someone who knows the field. Research can be done independently, but a professional should be by your side when purchasing. It can either be recommended by your acquaintances or chosen based on your judgment.

4. Determine the type of financing you need: Consider different loan options and programs to determine which one is best for you. Ensure you know all the conditions, costs, fees, taxes, and other charges. The more you investigate all this, the more prepared you will be to face it in an orderly manner.

5. If you don't like debt (like me) consider a different plan. Start a business, generate extra revenue and use that to buy a property. Then rent out that property and generate more revenue. There are some very useful real estate podcasts out there for the more business minded.

6. Keep an open mind: Don't get hung up on your first option. If you are close to a first choice that you liked, the disappointment may be great if it fails to materialize, and you may also miss out on other options you may end up liking more. This attitude will help you

face difficulties and setbacks throughout the search and purchase process.

7. Buy when you are sure: It is not a good idea to make a hasty decision, so make sure you have done all the necessary research.

In the United States, buying your first home is easier than you might think, and you don't need to have large savings or a high income. Some of the programs to consider are:

- HomeReady and Home Possible: These are loans with very low initial payment requirements, close to 3% of the price of the house.

- USDA mortgage loan: This allows you to finance 100% of the house's value without making a down payment. It is aimed at houses in rural areas.

- FHA mortgage loans: They are easy to qualify for, as they can be accessed with better credit scores or higher levels of debt.

- Prefabricated and mobile homes: They are one of the affordable homes and, in many cases, can be financed with conventional mortgage programs.

- Mortgage Credit Certificates: With these, you can object to a tax credit corresponding to a percentage of the interest on your mortgage.

- Down payment assistance: These are grants or loans specific for certain "neglected" or "developing" areas in which income level is not considered.

- Personal loans: They can be used to buy a house at a lower price.

These options can serve as starting points to help you determine which one best fits your situation, and then you can dive deeper by consulting a specialist with more knowledge on the subject.

The fact that you know that options may be within your reach and that you understand what they are about is a good start.

How to choose an insurance plan

Health insurance is very important. If you're already 26 years old, you're no longer covered by your parent's plan. You will need to choose the plan that's right for you.

What should I look for?

- Options: When you compare plans, consider the total costs, including premiums and out-of-pocket costs.

- Quality care: Access to personalized medical treatment no matter where you are.

- Discounted rates: You want in-network doctor and hospital options so you can take advantage of discounted rates.

- Annual checkups and preventive care at no extra cost. Preventive care, like annual exams and checkups, helps keep you healthy.

- Easy to use tools: Online tools can help you choose plans, find doctors, and predict costs.

- 24/7 service: When in doubt, you'll want to be able to talk to health care experts and access your claims.

What's 401k?

In the USA, this is an employer-sponsored retirement plan that is eligible for employees where they can make salary reduction contributions before or after taxes. The 401k plan allows employees to save and invest part of the income before taxes are deducted.

Employers offering the plan to their employees may elect to match individual contributions to the plan on behalf of their employees. They can also add a profit-sharing feature to the plan. You need to know that taxes are not paid until the money is withdrawn from the account.

Part 5: EXTRAS - What you need to know!

OK we've covered a lot so far! Here are some extra tips to bear in mind as you begin your life as an adult!

What you need to know about your car

In today's world, getting a car and learning to drive it is easy, but the tough part is understanding how it works and maintaining it. Therefore, here are ten things you need to know to drive safely and maintain your car.

1. *Engine oil*

People mistakenly believe that oil burns fuel in the car, but its primary function is to lubricate, cool, and clean the engine. Therefore, three things can happen to your car if you don't have enough oil: thermal degradation, oxidation, and compression heating. This will cause the oil to do the opposite of what it was designed to do, creating more friction, heating the engine, and building up dirt deposits.

2. *Spare tire*

The last thing you want is to change your flat tire and realize that your spare is also flat. The spare tire is not designed to be a decorative item on your car. It is there in case you experience a flat tire. Therefore, always keep a jack and other tools in the trunk of your car for when you need to change the tire. Checking if the spare part is in perfect working order is also a good idea.

How to change a tire

1. Find a safe location

2. Turn on your hazard lights

3. Apply the parking brake

4. Apply wheel wedges

5. Remove the hubcap or wheel cover

6. Loosen the lug nuts

7. Place the jack under the vehicle

8. Raise the vehicle with the jack

9. Unscrew the lug nuts

10. Remove the flat tire

11. Mount the spare tire on the lug bolts

12. Tighten the lug nuts by hand

13. Lower the vehicle and tighten the lug nuts again

14. Lower the vehicle completely

15. Replace the hubcap

16. Stow all equipment

17. Check the pressure in the spare tire

18. Take your flat tire to the garage.

3. *Wiper washer*

Windshield wipers are a necessity that many people tend to overlook. If you want to keep your windshield wipers in better condition, ensure the rubbers are in good shape and the correct size. You should generally replace them every six months, though it's best to check how often your car's manual suggests changing.

4. *Headlights and taillights*

Headlights and taillights dim over time, so it is recommended that you inspect them from time to time. Checking them is a preventive security measure and prevents you from being stopped by the police or a traffic officer. It is generally recommended to change the headlights every year.

5. *General car maintenance*

Regular car maintenance varies depending on the make and model. The best way to know the ideal maintenance plan for your car is to read the owner's manual, as it will give you the ideal service intervals for your car.

6. *Shock absorbers*

Does your car rock from time to time? Can you hear a screeching noise when you brake or go over a bump or pothole? Then your shock absorbers are probably worn out. This is one of the most common issues with older vehicles, so if you drive a car that's a couple of years old, check your shock absorbers.

7. *Air filter*

It is important to change air filters every six months. When engines get dirty, they can get clogged, so they have to work harder, and this can cause an increase in fuel consumption.

8. *Emergency kit*

You never know when your car might break down, and if it does, then you should have an emergency kit on hand:

- A properly inflated spare tire, wheel wrench, and tripod jack
- Jumper cables
- Tool kit and a multipurpose utility tool

- Flashlight and extra batteries

- Reflective triangles and brightly colored cloth to make your vehicle more visible

- Compass

- First aid kit with gauze, tape, bandages, antibiotic ointment, aspirin, a blanket, non-latex gloves, scissors, hydrocortisone, thermometer, tweezers, and instant cold compress

- Nonperishable, high-energy foods, such as unsalted nuts, dried fruits, and hard candy

- Drinking water

- Reflective vest in case you need to walk to get help

- Car charger for your cell phone

- Fire extinguisher

- Duct tape

- Rain poncho

- Additional items for cold weather include a snow brush, shovel, windshield washer fluid, warm clothing, cat litter for traction, and a blanket.

9. *Brakes*

Brakes are a safety feature that you should never overlook. Watch if the steering wheel jerks as you apply the brake pedals when driving. This could affect your car's stability control system and ABS (Anti-lock Braking System).

10. *Get a good mechanic*

And lastly, get a good mechanic. A good, honest, and knowledgeable mechanic is hard to come by, but if you find one, trust him firmly. Ask friends and family for their recommendations. Don't pick the first one you find to give you low rates. Take your time. You are putting the safety and performance of your car in their hands, so make sure they are good at what they are doing.

What you need to know about traveling

Whether you are a frequent or occasional traveler, having some of the following tips in mind can make things a little easier. Although you may find some of these suggestions obvious, you should still consider them.

Airline miles

If you are traveling a long distance and you are not a member of any frequent flyer programs, consider joining one of them. Collecting miles is a great way to get discounts on shopping, hotels, and more offers.

Sometimes these programs, like certain credit cards, give the right to use airport VIP lounges, spaces with exclusive paid or free services, depending on the case.

Beware: cheap can be expensive

Before booking a flight or reserving a hotel, do not get carried away exclusively by the price. Assess the consequences of your decisions. Sometimes the cheap option turns out to be expensive. Due to lack of public transportation, cheap tickets purchased off-peak may force you to take a taxi, pay more for your luggage than anticipated, or spend more on food while traveling. The same can happen to you with a hotel far from the center or a vehicle rental.

On a long-haul flight, paying a little more and traveling comfortably in a seat with more legroom or care service may be preferable.

Documents

Time is the most important thing when traveling. The earlier you book a flight, the cheaper it will be. By checking your documents early, you'll have more time to organize them. Make sure, for example, that your passport is valid. You will need more than six months left on your passport in many countries.

In addition, check if a visa is necessary even if you have been to your destination before since their immigration policy may have changed. In some countries, you can apply for a visa electronically, but in others, you must go to the consulate or embassy in person. The process can take weeks.

Before leaving your home, ensure you have the documentation in order.

Take a photo of the passport. Then save it to your phone and cloud using a password, so if you need it when you are away from home, you can find it easily.

The suitcase

Although it is basic advice, we tend to ignore it. Do not travel with excess baggage. Remember to pack only necessary items and forget about things you might not even use. Be sure to select clothing that can be combined. Choose footwear that is appropriate for the weather (and comfortable), and take accessories and technology items you won't find at the destination and might need. And if you're going overseas, don't forget your phone charger and adapter for that country.

Once you are sure about what you are taking with you, try to place everything in the suitcase in a way that takes up as little space as possible.

Bank and money

Although it may seem silly initially, the increase in identity theft is a serious threat, so it is worth telling your bank or credit card issuer that you will be traveling.

Additionally, it is always a good idea to notify your credit card company when traveling since some even offer free health coverage. Finally, it's important to know the local currency and whether credit cards are accepted where you are traveling to.

Telephone strategy

Find out about your company's telephony conditions if you travel outside your country. To avoid unpleasant surprises when you receive your bill, check the roaming rates and follow the operator's instructions. Getting a local SIM card for your phone may be a good idea if your travel plans do not involve frequent travel. You can often purchase one online in advance. Using online messaging services like Zoom and whatsapp can be a great choice.

Health

Finding out in advance about the health system of the destination and where you can go is necessary. If you have health insurance, check what cover it includes abroad. Read the small print; you can get more than one shock. Health is expensive in many countries and poor in others. An insurance that covers all the guarantees and saves your trip can save your economy. If you live in Europe and will be traveling to another European country, apply for a free E111 form.

In terms of health, we need to consider our destination's policy. Find out in advance what vaccinations and health conditions are required for admission.

Finally, do not assume that abroad you will find common medicines with the same ease as here. They may be cheaper, infinitely more expensive, or they simply do not exist. Just in case, prepare your first aid kit.

Check the weather forecasts

This is not a minor matter, a few days before your trip, check the weather forecast. Plan ahead.

Free tours

Today, many tourist cities worldwide offer "free" tours you can find and book online. This type of tour is nice since the guides are usually locals who not only know the history and interesting facts about the place but also know where to eat and how to move around (and they share that information with the group). While they are not free, you just need to tip your guide at the end of the tour to rate his work.

What you need to know about social media

As long as we utilize them wisely, these digital channels will positively impact our lives. Therefore, to improve our relationship with Social Media, here are some tips to help us make the most of them and take advantage of all they offer.

Put down your phone

In the last few years, mobile phone usage has gone from 33% to 50.1%, i.e., half of the time spent online is through mobile devices. In this sense, the mobile is the main means of access to social networks. Be aware of how much time you spend on your phone. When you are old, one thing you'll never wish that you spent more time on your phone scrolling through social media!

Work on technological independence

Technological dependence is a real issue today. There are approximately 8.6 accounts on social networks per person around the world, and most are accessed through mobile devices.

Most people can't go more than an hour without looking at their phones, with 61% saying they check them first in the morning and the last thing at night.

The key to becoming more independent of technology is understanding what works best for you and your health and daily routine. There are endless options, like turning off your phone earlier to spend more time with friends or turning it on later to read something you enjoy while eating breakfast.

Limit the use of social networks.

Be aware of how much time you spend on social media. According to statistics, the average user of social networks spends two hours and twenty-four minutes per day on social networks. As an effective way to limit the amount of time the user spends on social networking sites, the time limit can be activated by social networks on the mobile device so that the user is more aware of how much time he wasted on his rambling before.

Follow quality accounts

You should ensure that your time on social media is spent on things that genuinely interest you, not on what is just noise. On social networks, become discerning with the accounts they follow. Remove accounts that make you feel sad or angry, or waste a lot of your time.

Identify the real stories

You should be aware that social media only displays a small part of a person and that reality is often much different. Many people believe that what is published on social media encompasses the entire life of influencers and brands. But, in reality, they show only a small portion of their daily lives. To avoid feeling frustrated when comparing their life with yours, you must be aware of this.

Use social media to get inspired and connect with others

Social networks allow you to discover new ideas, and ways of seeing and acting. These new social networks provide a source of inspiration for users by letting them imitate, add, and create content from original videos of their role models. Tik Tok videos, for example, receive an average of 17 billion views per month. This video social network has the highest social media engagement rate per post.

For brands, however, it is a new way to advertise their products and services more intimately than with a traditional ad. Pinterest has also become a great window for users who discover a large network of environments and trends they can duplicate in reality.

Engage friends and family via social media

With the advent of mobile phones, mobile networks have become the means of communication between friends and family. Mobile phones are used 70% by people to communicate with their closest friends and family through applications, social networks, or calls. Most mobile users only communicate via instant messaging applications or social networks. Social media platforms offer an immediacy that would otherwise be lacking.

Be empathic

With the pandemic, we have seen the need to support one another. It has demonstrated how vulnerable we are as a species, no matter our status, ethnicity, nationality, or sex.

We are all human, and we all have stories to tell. Understanding this is key to being responsible on social media. We can be proactive, assertive, and empathetic instead of joining the hate, ridicule, and criticism sweeping the world.

Conclusion

As children and teenagers, we were usually told where to go and what to do, by our parents, by our teachers in school and by adults. We didn't have a lot of choices. Instead there was a path we were expected to follow. Now as an adult, our lives are very different! And with the tips and strategies in this book you are now prepared to take on the world!

You've learned how to find a job, fix your car, live away from home and manage your money effectively. You understand how important it is to eat healthy, take care of your body, wear SPF and exercise.

You've discovered why it's good to make more money than you spend, make new friends to enrich your life, maybe even start your own business!

One of the most important lessons I learned in my life was to follow my gut and do more of what I love. If you are in a situation where your gut is saying something is off... listen to what your body is telling you. And that goes for a house share, a job or a night out in the city.

Figure out what you love. If you love art, don't give it up. Maybe you need an office job to pay the bills, but follow your dreams and keep painting on the weekends.

I truly hope that reading this book has greatly benefited you and helped you have great success and happiness in life as an adult. You can quickly implement the lessons you learned in your daily life and notice the positive effects.

Before you go, I have a small request to make. I would really appreciate it if you could review this book and share your lessons learned. Doing so will help me a lot in getting this book out to other young adults who can benefit from the tips and strategies I have shared.

We only get one chance to live our lives. Dream big and don't have any regrets.

You've got this!

References

Hu, Y., Shmygelska, A., Tran, D., Eriksson, N., Tung, J. Y., & Hinds, D. A. (2016). GWAS of 89,283 individuals identifies genetic variants associated with self-reporting of being a morning person. *Nature communications, 7*(1), 1-9.

www.ingramcontent.com/pod-product-compliance
Lightning Source LLC
Chambersburg PA
CBHW071554080526
44588CB00010B/905